ONE PROVEN STEP TO LIVE
IMPOSSIBLE POTENTIAL

THAD KUNTZ

Library of Congress Control Number: 2021908420

The capitalization format for pronouns in this book is meant to follow the most authoritative traditional English. This resource is also available online as a free ebook and in high-quality audio. For more information or to order additional printed copies, email your requests to kuntzbooks@gmail.com.

CONTENTS

INTRODUCTION

We sat onboard the Airbus A330 at the Nadi Airport in Fiji and waited. Through the window we could see cargo containers being loaded and unloaded from the plane holds, and it seemed to be a very slow process. My older brother, Kelly, and I had more than 5,000 miles of open ocean between us and Los Angeles, and we were in no position to make our trip happen any sooner. We were still on "Fiji Time," and that was our option.

Kelly was seated a few rows up, and I started into conversation with the passenger seated beside me. Ashwin was a Hindu man in his mid-20s who had spent his life in Fiji. This trip was a huge milestone for him, and he was excited and chatty. We talked about his job and our travel plans for a good while, and we got to know each other pretty well before the plane took off.

During our 10-hour transit over the Pacific, Ashwin and I began discussing his Hindu beliefs. After I initiated the topic, he was not hesitant to discuss it openly. He explained his view of karma to me, and how reasonable it was that we eventually get what we deserve. After trying to understand his personal vision for a while, it became obvious that Ashwin's hope was good karma in his next life. So I asked him what he would do if he realized that he had done wrong. And surprisingly, he had a very specific regiment of fasting that he believed could amend the wrong. But he was also clear that fasting was not a solution for larger evils.

So, out of curiosity, I asked what happens if you keep doing bad things without regard to karma. He simply said, "You would go to Hell." I was a bit taken aback by his reply and asked him whether a person could recover from such a life of bad deeds and avoid Hell. He said with conviction, "No." We talked some more about reincarnation and many other Hindu concepts, but there was a burning inside of me to share the light of the Gospel.

Eventually we found our way to the Law of Moses, and as Ashwin heard the Ten Commandments, his conscience began convincing him of those truths and of his own guilt in relation to them. He began to realize that he had, in fact, attained a larger debt and needed help that Hinduism could not provide. I told him about the man, Jesus of Nazareth, and how his substitutionary death was anticipated for thousands of years. And as Ashwin heard these things his conscience seemed to cry out. He wanted to know more. He seemed to hunger for the help of a Messiah and even began praying audibly to that end while still seated beside me somewhere over the Pacific Ocean.

Why would this man—after so many years of Hinduism—desire another way? Why would he move so quickly from his confidence in karma to seeking Jesus of Nazareth? There is a simple answer to these questions that touches every human being on the planet. If you will take a few moments to read through the pages of this little book, you will be deeply enriched in understanding that answer.

CHAPTER 1:
You Can

One of the great pleasures of parenting is planting and nurturing seeds of confidence in a young life. Children thrive on words of encouragement and actions that express genuine interest. We all do. And there is good reason to set our hopes high. Human achievement in the 21st century is so jaw-dropping that it is difficult even to imagine any hard limits. We can travel around the world at our leisure and store 10 million books on a keychain in our pocket. The potential of children and young adults in our technologically advanced generation seems boundless. What a joy it is to fuel that courage.

Origins of human potential
The actions of an insightful parent or educator can spark an interest that lasts a lifetime and makes history. Simple earnest words of support can shape a life, echoing in the mind and soul of a person across decades.[1] Even the boldest of us sometimes need an uplifting word to boost our spirits. After facing the immense challenges of the American Civil War and

distinguishing himself as one of the great leaders of all time, President Abraham Lincoln was assassinated on April 14, 1865. Tucked in his wallet were several folded newspaper clippings, many of which were complimentary of his leadership decisions. After all his victories and accomplishments, Lincoln still found solace in those encouraging words.

Where is your bar set? And how was your bar set where it is? These are essential questions that we cannot afford to neglect. Our perceived limits have precise origins and broad outgrowths that we ought to explore aggressively.[2] Henry Ford humorously said, "Whether you think you can, or think you can't, you're right." Natural limits are real (most of us will never run a 4-minute mile), but too often we short ourselves by a simple lack of vision.[3]

Often shortsightedness traces back to an early criticism or unkind word that tarnished the hopes of a child or young adult.[4] In some cases, well-meaning doctors have hastily and imprecisely diagnosed patients. This is a special risk for mental health professionals who can pronounce diagnoses even without clear physical evidence. One in six adults in America uses a mood-altering drug, and many others have been given labels that provide little but discouragement for their hopes. Mental illnesses are serious, but there is hope for every condition in this life.[5] Sadly, even the best of doctors can fail to see the larger context of that hope.

People are much more than statistics. Living human beings have living potential that is not generic.[6] No amount of charting or written descriptions can do a person justice.[7] (Even the best biographies about a person should not be confused with the truth of the person himself or herself.) Life consists of more than a mechanical body, and to be human is a great privilege that we should never underestimate.

Human potential goes far beyond physical strength and brain power. Each of us has a personality that is truly unique.[8] We also have the potential to value other personalities and principles of right and wrong. We can appreciate values such as justice, mercy, beauty, and love. And—whether for better or for worse— internal values are what undergird all we do.[9] We do whatever we think is most important; and if nothing is important to us, then we will tend to do nothing.[10] What is important to one person may seem like a waste to another, and it is a person's unique personality that determines what is most important to him or her.[11]

Internal values are real and powerful. They are, in fact, among the most outstanding evidence that we are more than a body. I recall a conversation I shared with an enthusiastic young atheist man one day.

"One thing I don't like about being an atheist," he said candidly, "is that when things go well, I don't have anyone to thank." This young man, Tyler, had been immersed in secular humanism, and although he was enthusiastic about it, he was still modest enough to recognize some providential gifts in his life. Tyler's willingness to appreciate these gifts was not taught by literature; it was an internal value that saw through the illogic of ingratitude.[12] Human potential is a gift.

The power of values

The greatest achievements in human history tend to sprout from human values.[13] Our values identify what is valuable (the words share a common root) and shape potential achievements to reach those things of value. If in the end there is no value, then there has been no achievement.[14] If our values are good, our life will lean toward good potential. And if our values are bad, our life will lean toward bad potential. Jesus of Nazareth taught this principle saying, "A good man out of the good treasure of the heart bringeth forth good things: and an evil man out of the evil treasure bringeth forth evil things."[15] So it is critical—if we hope to shape the future for the better—that we identify and adopt good values.

We all have values that we live by. There are virtually no exceptions to this rule. Even those with severe mental disabilities tend to prefer certain things over others. The question is not "if values?" but "what values?" When we disbelieve or become irreligious, we are simply adopting new values. We may prefer values that are not clearly articulated in the form of a doctrinal statement, but we must have values.[16] The huge achievements of outspoken irreligious minds would not be possible aside from some tenacious values. And it would be wise for those who are irreligious to evaluate why they value what they do. This becomes more difficult, however, when values are not clearly articulated.

It is also important to note that a person's values are not necessarily consistent with what that person associates with publicly.[17] For instance, we may say that we value prayer deeply, but our practice of it may reveal otherwise. It is much easier to build a façade of strong values than it is to genuinely adopt them. And it is easier still to adopt stealthy or tentative values for which we cannot be held accountable.[18] There are myriads of ways to obscure our personal values, and there can be some good reasons to do so. As a rule though, the more we shed light on our values the better we can understand them and the more we can improve them.[19] Hypocrisy and inconsistency in our values tend to be destructive, and we should consider this point very mindfully. Values can build, and they can destroy.

Meditation defines values
The desire to shed light on our values and to improve them is not an empty hope. For thousands of years

eastern mystics and descendants of Abraham have sought to understand themselves through the valuable practice of mindfulness meditation. When Abraham's son Isaac first encountered his bride, he was walking in an open field "to meditate."[20] And the practice of meditation can be easily traced back another 19 generations before Abraham to the second chapter of Genesis.[21]

Various Vedic traditions tracing to the Indus Valley—now Pakistan—may have also practiced mindfulness meditation since roughly the time of Abraham (4,000 years ago). Vedic writings describing such practices date back perhaps as far as 3,000 years ago. These Vedic traditions became the basis of modern Hinduism—one of the oldest religions in the world.

Jewish Scriptures teach the principle of meditation and encourage it, but Hinduism and other related traditions such as Buddhism place an extreme emphasis on the practice and seem to take meditation to its limits. Hinduism and Buddhism place a high value on seeking the most appropriate path and walking it diligently. According to these and other similar traditions, the path must be determined on an individual basis, and there is no universally right path. Each person must find his or her own path or "dharma" as it is called. This requires deep meditation—not only to discover the right path, but to pursue it with focus. Unlike typical eastern philosophies, however, Judaism provides a defined path that followers can seek to attain.[22]

By starting with clear written principles, Judaism can help focus the practice of meditation and allow individuals to make the most of it.[23] Just as we require a mind and body to start the process of meditation, there may be good reasons to believe that we require sound *principles* to focus our meditation effectively.

Regardless of the specific approach used, meditation clearly offers some benefits, and there are some great lessons to learn from it.[24] Our natural intuitions are powerful, but they can become clouded or overlooked easily in the business of life.[25] Mindfulness allows us to tap into those deeper intuitions and more accurately identify both our values and emotions.

Feeling a solution

Emotional intelligence is that critical skill of learning our own intuitions and understanding our emotional responses so that we can better relate to others.[26] The concept of emotional intelligence (EI) was made popular by Daniel Goleman in his book *Emotional Intelligence: Why it can matter more than IQ*. Goleman explores some of the structures and processes that make EI possible. One fascinating group of these structures—known as the basal ganglia—is found deep in the brain. Goleman explains:

> Our life wisdom on any topic is stored in the basal ganglia. The basal ganglia is so primitive that it has zero connectivity to the verbal cortex. It can't tell us what it knows in words. It tells us in feelings, it has a lot of connectivity to the emotional centers of the brain and to the gut. It tells us this is right or this is wrong as a gut feeling.

Despite the elusive nature of these gut feelings, we can become aware of them and even define them through mindfulness. We can in effect learn to read the sign language of our own body and define it in very practical terms.[27]

We are all born with certain instincts, but our gut feelings are fine-tuned through experiences that we build up over the course of years.[28] And in order to draw out those gut feelings, we need to think of precise scenarios that apply to those feelings. Those scenarios can be learned through certain life events or by a combination of life events and established wisdom.[29]

The advantage of wisdom

Eastern Mysticism tends to rely primarily on meditation and life events, whereas Judaism relies heavily on established wisdom *confirmed* by meditation and life events. By starting with a foundation of established wisdom, Judaism can logically aim to make the most of meditation—even though Judaism emphasizes meditation less compared to Hinduism, Buddhism, etc.[30]

It is possible for a person with no clear boundaries to wander aimlessly in meditation while searching for an unclear path. And it is also possible— probable in fact—that a person seeking an unclear path will settle for less than her full potential. If we are not aiming for anything in particular, ending well would be more of a surprise than a logical expectation.[31] These are a few reasons that established wisdom provides an important aid to meditation.

Even though meditation is a great tool for personal development, it is an imperfect means, and not an end in itself.[32] If criminal violence is premeditated, for instance, it is worse than if it is committed on the spur of the moment. The real key to good meditation is the quality of what we meditate on.[33] And without good aims, we will tend to go astray at some point.

For this reason, Abrahamic religions tend to place a high value on sacred writings.[34] Both Judaism and Islam emphasize what they consider to be established wisdom, and some major portions of their holy books even overlap. Many sacred writings exist around the world, and determining which of them—if any—is reliable requires study and meditation. Our natural gut feeling (conscience) can help confirm or disconfirm the authenticity of various sacred writings, *if* we will seek for it legitimately. The key word of course being "if." Jesus of Nazareth taught this when he said "Ask, and it shall be given you; seek, and ye shall find; knock, and it shall be opened unto you."[35]

In traditional Jewish culture, it was common for boys and girls to memorize the Pentateuch by age 13.[36] Early in the 1st century an average young Jew could have the nearly 80,000 words of the Torah committed to memory and be very familiar with the rest of the Jewish Scriptures. This was only the first level of Jewish education known as *Bet Sefer*, and the choicest of these students would continue to much more challenging levels of study.

In the 14th century, Islam began a similar tradition of Hafiz. It is estimated that millions of Muslims have committed the nearly 78,000 words of the Quran—traditionally printed in 604 pages of Arabic text—to memory. Although these practices are relatively uncommon in the 21st century, it is important to note that such feats are by no means superhuman.

When Jesus walked the streets of Nazareth, a typical representative of the culture could identify an accurate quote from any of the Jewish Scriptures. A public speaker could simply begin a quote with "It is written" knowing that most of his audience would be able to recall the passage from memory.[37]

In our fast-paced culture we tend to cringe at the thought of such a time-consuming work, but most of us are well capable of it. And being immersed in our culture of information overload, it is almost certain that most of us have already stored the Torah's equivalent of useless information in mind. We have far more potential than we realize, and wisdom helps us reach it.

Life is an asset

The real question is not whether we are capable of reaching greater potential, but whether we care enough about our own life to invest in it like that.[38] Though we may feel that we place a very high value on our life, the way we invest our time and attention often reveals otherwise. What does your life mean to you? Is your life equivalent to the things you own? We know intuitively that life is important, and that it is something more than pleasures and possessions.

So each of us ought to ask this simple question: What am I doing to appreciate my life?[39]

Life is real, and it is a great treasure.[40] If we fail to identify the value of life itself, we are directly eroding our potential. The accomplishments of a lifetime are, in fact, empty unless we appreciate life itself. If life has no value, the legacy of a life cannot be anything but

irrelevant. We must see the value of our own life before
we can reach the potential of our life. And although it
seems simple enough to recognize the value of life,
there can be many obstacles.

One day there was a short tax collector who was
trying to get a look at Jesus of Nazareth. The streets in
Jericho were busy that day; and although he was close,
this man Zacchaeus could not see much of anything.
He was resourceful, however, and didn't hesitate to
climb a nearby tree to get a view. And sure enough,
Zacchaeus saw the man he was looking for. Jesus was
walking toward the tree and ended up speaking to
Zacchaeus personally. That small man soon experienced
a big turning point in his life, but it was only after he
rose above the immediate distractions.[41]

We are so prone to get lost in the shuffle of
things around us and to miss the greater opportunities
in life.[42] Imagine raising a child and leaving him with a
fortune, but no meaningful relationship with you. That
happens too often.

Like Zacchaeus we can rise above the
distractions, but it will not happen as a passive process.
Jesus of Nazareth emphasized our need for a high level
of focus in this area saying, "Take heed, and beware of
covetousness: for a man's life consisteth not in the
abundance of the things which he possesseth."[43]

We must first acknowledge the value of life,
and then position ourselves to appreciate it. Our

possessions are not the most valuable things in life, nor are they the most reliable. What seems like a great achievement one day may become a faded memory the next.[44]

Jeff Bezos, the founder and CEO of Amazon, was named the richest person on earth in 2017, and held the title till January 2021. His simple-yet-effective philosophy has been to treat every day like "day one." In other words, he sees the benefit in always treating his business like a startup and avoiding an attitude of stasis. Jeff has seen some outstanding success in his business, but the benefit of his simple philosophy applies to things much more valuable than financial gain.[45]

A healthy child has a natural enthusiasm about life, and we could all learn a lot from it. Age has a way of clouding that enthusiasm, and we often suffer because of it. As we grow older, we experience much evil in the world and may easily come to expect more evil.[46] Children generally lack these reservations and often develop more rapidly as a result. They expect to learn new things every day and are eager to grow.

A healthy child sees forward progress as the only reasonable option; he does not want to live his life forever in the first grade. There is, of course, nothing noble about being naïve or making unnecessary blunders, but the point is to learn from the irrepressible courage and curiosity of youth. We ought to live with our eyes open to the real world, but it is possible also to value and maintain youthful interests for many years along the way.[47] Life is a wonderful asset to have.

A heart to overcome

American rock climber Alex Honnold had a passion for climbing as a child and, by age 10, was practicing it at a local gym several times a week. As a teenager he entered many rock-climbing championships and did well, but he would by no means consider himself extraordinary. "I was never, like, a bad climber, but I was never a great climber either," he says. "Because there were a lot of other climbers who were much, much stronger than me, who started as kids and were, like, instantly freakishly strong… They just have, like, a natural gift. And that was never me." Alex was clearly fascinated by climbing as a child and has continued to pursue that interest into his adult years.

That irrepressible fascination with climbing has allowed him to do things that are unique in human history. On Saturday morning June 3, 2017, Alex Honnold successfully ascended El Capitan—an enormous granite monolith that is the center of the rock climbing universe—with no ropes or protective gear ("free solo"). His historic climb has been defined by many as one of the greatest athletic achievements of all time. For a climber who considers his abilities more average than extraordinary, he apparently has a bit to teach all of us about potential.

One of the simplest lessons that we can glean from Alex's feat is the power of sincere interest: "I just loved climbing," he recalls. "And I've been climbing all the time ever since."

Having a love for the things we do expands our potential.[48] It really is that simple. If Alex was indifferent about rock climbing, he could be easily stumped by even the simplest climbs; and his ability to focus his mind and body to recall and overcome the many details of a rock face would be severely weakened. He can do what he does because he cares about it.

Alex cared enough about the big climb to spend many hundreds of hours practicing it. He had free-climbed El Capitan with safety ropes about 9 years before his famous free solo climb. But leading up to his famous climb, Alex spent day after day and month after month mastering that enormous granite face. There is no doubt that his love for rock climbing drove this man to such an extraordinary level of dedication. And through such outstanding dedication, Alex developed a level of confidence on which he would stake his very life.

From Alex Honnold's experience we can learn several lessons. Our potential is greater than most of us realize, and if we are going to reach that greater potential, we should first care to reach it. We can say that we are too busy for family or too busy for spiritual things, but the reality is that we can make time for what matters. We are prone at times to make excuses rather than make things happen. Yes we have limits, but it is important to remember that not every mile marker is the finish line. We can go farther and live more, if we have a heart to do so.

Before we move forward, it is critical that we see our potential realistically. This is the whole point here. If we stop short of our natural potential, we are going to have a very hard time understanding and appreciating things beyond that potential.[49] Too many of us are content to live far below our best and then make excuses for it. This is a harmful tendency that we need to root out of our lives. No doubt there are vast galaxies beyond our natural potential, but let's be real about what we *can* do. We ought to make an honest effort to do what we can, and then we can talk about what we cannot do, and why it matters.

CHAPTER 2:
The Storm Before the Calm

Cool air and dense clouds began moving into Budapest as Fall 1973 arrived. Summer's heat had quickly dissolved into a memory, and the bold colors of a changing landscape now burst to life. A young father walked beside his little girl with warm enthusiasm, unbroken by the cold communist regime that gripped his country. Laszlo was eager to see his controversial theory put to the test, and his spry 4-year-old could hardly be any more excited about it.

They made their way through the city streets to an unlikely destination—Voros Meteor, a local chess club known to attract some high-level, formidable players from around the country and even beyond. A cloud of tobacco smoke greeted them as they entered the main room full of veteran chess players competing aggressively—many even making wagers on the matches. Laszlo and his girl could hear the sound of chess pieces being slapped around the boards, and it was obvious that these men were engaged in hot competition.

When Laszlo introduced his 4-year-old, Susan, to some of the veteran players and asked if she could play a game, it seemed comical. But some of them decided to go ahead and humor her for a game anyway. To almost everyone's surprise, she played like a boss! Susan—the cute little 4-year-old girl—won against men who had played for decades. Suddenly these men were confronted by a very awkward reality.

One after another the men offered excuses for their loss: "I didn't sleep enough last night" or "I'm not feeling well" or "my stomach is hurting." Laszlo had trained a powerful little chess player through some months of intense study and energetic practice, but her surprising skill was hard for her victims to appreciate. The men she defeated all seemed to be suffering from some ailment or another, and over time Susan Polgar—who would later become a world-renowned Grandmaster—began to reflect on whether she would *ever* beat a "healthy" man.

We are all prone to deny reality when it embarrasses us.[1] But often it is the very things that shame us that also expose the greatest opportunities for our growth.[2] The road to improvement requires the gravel of shortcomings. And if we fail to recognize our shortcomings, we will guarantee ourselves a shortened potential.[3] Embracing truth excavates that gravel and breaks up our clods of conceit. Learning to see our own shortcomings as they really are is a simple and reasonable concept; but the actual practice of it is far from simple, so long as humans are involved. We tend to bury them.

What foundation?

The novelist J. K. Rowling had come to a low point in her life in December 1993. After a turbulent marriage ended abruptly, Rowling was a single mother with no job and very little money. She saw herself as a huge failure and began falling into depression. But as she wrestled with it all, she made a surprising discovery. She realized that there was actually a benefit to experiencing her failures and that recognizing her failures liberated her to rebuild.

Rowling's failures had, in fact, cleared some space in her life to move forward. Though she was correct and wise to see the benefit in it, she still may have missed the best opportunity she had. Rowling said ironically, "Rock bottom became the solid foundation on which I rebuilt my life." When life fell apart for Rowling, she saw her foundation through the wreckage and decided to rebuild on the same spot. Rowling set a great example of accepting her shortcomings, but her most fundamental shortcoming was left buried and built upon. When a person's life implodes, rock bottom does not become a solid foundation; rock bottom tends to reveal the flawed foundation that needs to be replaced.[4]

Many would disagree that Rowling made a mistake in rebuilding on her own rock bottom, but what she produced in the years that followed was compromised at best. Thanks to J. K Rowling, children around the world have taken a greater interest in the evils of defiance and manipulation.[5] There is no doubt that Rowling has a highly gifted mind for writing; but her foundation has at times proven uncertain, and she could attest to that. In 2007 after achieving international fame for her children's novels, Rowling had become quite wealthy, and quite depressed. Rowling said that people looking for help came after her like a tsunami and she found herself overwhelmed and at "rock bottom" again.

If life looks empty and broken, there is a good opportunity—and good reason—to inspect our foundation before moving forward. If we then choose to build on that same foundation and in time find ourselves back at rock bottom, it is most probably more than a coincidence.[6]

When 4-year-old Susan Polgar played her first chess tournament in 1974, she won all 10 games that she played. Given those results, it would be most logical for her opponents to recognize her skill rather than to make excuses. In the same way, crumbling foundations can be ignored for a while, but patches and remodels above such will fail predictably.

We all have shortcomings, of course, but don't we like to think that our shortcomings are more trivial than foundational? The reality may be more uncomfortable than that. It is difficult even to entertain the thought of it—but it is possible—that we are spending our lives on a condemned foundation. We see hairline cracks here and there leading to larger fractures in the corners; uneven floors begin to give way, and we scramble to redeem our splintering joists. We labor with diligence to build our lives well, but what are we building on? Have we dug down deeply enough to get past loose clay and shifting sands to build life on a solid foundation? There is such a thing, and we would be wise to pursue it.[7]

Really search inside yourself

Chade-meng Tan—or simply "Meng" as he likes to be known—joined Google in 2000 as a software engineer, and through surprising circumstances has become one of the major thought leaders of our time. Meng was hired to write code and develop software for Google, but after seven years of engineering work there, he began "Search Inside Yourself"—a personal growth program based on emotional intelligence and mindfulness. In 2012 he wrote a New York Times bestselling book with the same title: *Search Inside Yourself.*

One of the many things we can learn from Meng is the importance of searching inside of ourselves. This is good practical wisdom if we are going to be real with ourselves and others.[8] Our culture is too rushed, and we are often simply out of touch with ourselves and many around us. Meng explains in great detail that there are both social and financial advantages to learning about ourselves and others, and those advantages are what he seems to enjoy speaking about most. What Meng does not explain, however, is that such motives are insincere, and what they produce is not healthy.[9] So while he is correct that we should search inside ourselves, Meng may have missed an even deeper bottom line.

Meng is known for his fun-loving, charismatic personality and unflappable sense of humor. His official title became "The Jolly Good Fellow," which was printed on his Google business card with the words "which nobody can deny" in parentheses beneath it. Meng has a magnetism about him. His office was covered with celebrity photos. Whenever a famous person would visit the Google campus, Meng would greet each one enthusiastically and ask to have his picture taken with the celebrity. He accumulated an impressive collection over the years, but never seemed to take his own fame too seriously—which is a great lesson for us all.[10] He encourages people to be silly and live happily. His Google title illustrates that well—it's hilarious. Meng can teach us a lot about the joys of being "jolly," but there is also a serious problem. He believes and teaches the "good" part quite literally, and it is not a healthy path to walk.

There is a great danger in assuming the good nature of a person. A doctor who tells a patient he is getting better can of course encourage that patient, but if the patient is in fact *not* getting better but needs critical medical help, the doctor's empty words without treatment will do more harm than good. Left unchecked most diseases progress, and that is exactly what happens when we assume that we are good-natured and pure.[11]

We could know better if we search inside ourselves objectively.[12] What seems harmless and innocent may very well be deceptive and deadly, and we would be wise to learn the local plants before eating the colorful fruits they offer.

The fun song lyrics on Meng's business card are a good case in point. The popular French folk song meaning "the death and burial of the Invincible Marlborough" provided the tune for the song "For He's a Jolly Good Fellow." The song was inspired by a false rumor. During the War of the Spanish Succession an incorrect report circulated in France that one of Spain's great military leaders, the Duke of Marlborough, was killed in September 1709 during one of the bloodiest battles of that war. Spain lost over 10,000 men in that battle, but Marlborough was not one of them. In response to this false report, a song spread through much of France mocking the death of Marlborough. Although it seems entirely innocent, the fun and simple tone of that song was actually meant to be sardonic—a mockery of the man's death.

The song was very familiar throughout France and even spread beyond for many years. It was likely the song that French Emperor Napoleon Bonaparte hummed while crossing the Neman River on his failed invasion of Russia in 1812—a campaign that claimed the lives of nearly 1 million men. Napoleon liked the tune and hummed it often. But he did not necessarily have a healthy mindset about the song.

Within a few decades of Napoleon's Russian invasion, the familiar tune was being sung in Europe and America with the words "For he's a jolly good fellow." And of course you would have to be a real grinch to doubt the accuracy of that rumor, since apparently "nobody can deny." Or—is it entirely *reasonable* to doubt the jolly-good-fellow theory?

It is fair to ask: If we are such lovely creatures, such jolly good fellows, why has evil tracked human history so tightly? Could it be that our nature is not so lovely after all?[13] But who wants to deal with that? Who wants to deal with foundational problems when we can just patch and paint? Our long-term potential, however, may depend on some deeper stuff. We may need some heavy demolition and a better foundation before we can move forward legitimately.

Meng's bestselling book *Search Inside Yourself* is not impartial about what you will discover inside. The author's premise is unmistakable. He assumes right away that we have to unveil the beauty within. He begins the book with a famous quote by Marcus Aurelius: "Look within; within is the fountain of all good."

Marcus Aurelius wrote this memorable quote in his work *Meditations* while beginning a fragile military campaign and seeking intensely to gain tactical advantage in it. To be fair, he was a more civil Roman emperor than many who had gone before. But pointing inside himself as an ultimate source of good seems irrational, and frankly, it is not credible.[14]

Marcus Aurelius was the first Roman Emperor to appoint a co-ruler to protect against the possibility of his assassination. He knew enough about Roman history and human nature to anticipate such a threat and take steps to mitigate it. Marcus also expressed a serious lack of confidence in his own cousin Lucius Verus whom he had appointed as co-ruler. Later when Marcus' son Commodus replaced Lucius as co-ruler, Marcus' relationship with his son began to crumble steadily. After Marcus' mysterious death in 180 A.D., his son Commodus led the Roman Empire into a period of major decline with a glaring lack of personal restraint.

In a broader sense, however, the Roman Empire was never known for humility and compassion. In fact, this empire raised the standard of cruelty and perfected human torture through inventions such as crucifixion. The 1st-century historian Tacitus was thoroughly unimpressed with Roman morality and defined the city of Rome as "[the place] whither all things horrible and disgraced flow from all quarters, as to a common receptacle, and where they are encouraged." So it is especially ironic that—of all men—a 2nd-century Roman emperor would point to his own essential nature as "the fountain of all things good."

It is so human for us to see the lack of credibility in a man like Marcus Aurelius, but then to assume we are better than that.[15] In July of 64 A.D. the city of Rome burned for nearly a week during the reign of Nero, who was accused of setting the fire himself. To deflect the rumor Nero laid blame on a small group known as Christians and tortured them to death. Often they were fastened to fire stakes and burned alive to light Nero's garden—providing a source of evening entertainment.

We gasp at such evil, but it is closer than we realize. The human genes and essential nature of a man don't change merely because 80 generations pass. We are Nero's children, or children of men like him.[16] A powerful and disturbing evidence of that fact is our tendency to shift blame.[17]

Roughly 33 years before the burning of Rome, Jesus of Nazareth said, "Woe unto you, scribes and Pharisees, hypocrites! because ye build the tombs of the prophets, and garnish the sepulchres of the righteous, And say, If we had been in the days of our fathers, we would not have been partakers with them in the blood of the prophets. Wherefore ye be witnesses unto yourselves, that ye are the children of them which killed the prophets."[18] This is where a real look inside will lead.

If the warts go deep

Seeing such a raw view of our pedigree is not pleasant. And to be fair, it is entirely human to repress such thoughts. It is overwhelming to consider the reality of our natural condition. Is it possible that we are not good by nature? We would like to think that regardless of how bad a person's actions appear, he or she is really a good person deep down; and of course *we* are good people deep down. But that may not be true; we may not be good by nature, deep down.[19]

Sin and evil are only too real, and our nature may well be deeply flawed.[20] Though we don't like to hear that, the truth can be nourishing to our essential health.[21]

Religions of every ilk tend to diminish, gloss over, or pseudo-solve this problem. To reach the greatest potential for our life, it is crucial that we grasp and fully embrace this truth. Sin and evil are real, and they are outgrowths of our own human nature.

Like most people in the world, Chade-meng Tan does not see himself as religious. He is a Buddhist and rarely speaks publicly without first setting up images of Buddha. He had a personal visit from the Dalai Lama for his 40th birthday. But he thinks of his beliefs as universal laws that transcend any religion. Meng believes that he lives free from religious bondage and is able to access a clear sense of reality through meditation and objective science. But Meng, like other Buddhists, forces an artificial ignorance about the reality of evil. His system has taught him to ignore or forget wrongs rather than correct them. Meng summarizes what he has learned from 27 years of Buddhist meditation as simply "letting go."

We all have a lot to learn about letting go, and there is great value and wisdom to it in the proper path.[22] But letting go of bad habits does not repair the trail of wreckage in their wake, and it does not replace them with right paths for us to move forward.[23] If the wrong runs deep in us, we must dig down and face it.

The cost of compassion

Meng speaks often and emphatically about the need for compassion in our lives. He emphasizes the joy that compassion will bring into our own lives and the lives of many others, and this is an amazing fact of life.[24] We do get joy from serving others. But if we are serving others with the goal of giving ourselves a boost, we are simply using others to accomplish our ends, and our compassion is no more than a hollow pretense.

Compassion means sharing in another's suffering.[25] So if our goal in life is to let go of all burdens, we cannot have genuine compassion because doing so would defeat our goal.

The stated goal of Buddhism is to end suffering, and that is a good logical goal. Seriously—who wants to suffer? We can definitely appreciate that goal and those who work to reduce suffering in the world. Wouldn't we all prefer a neighbor whose stated goal is reducing our suffering over one who is bent on being a pain in the neck? Of course we would. But do Buddhism and other "happy" religions actually lead to real compassion (shared suffering)?

Logically they cannot.

Real friends know how to share our load.[26] They do not throw away our burdens, they shoulder them. This is what motivated Jesus of Nazareth. We see his rule of life summed up in the book of Galatians:

"Bear ye one another's burdens, and so fulfil the law of Christ."[27] This is our challenge!

Seven centuries before Jesus was born in Bethlehem, the prophet Isaiah anticipated such a compassionate work when he wrote: "Surely he hath borne our griefs, and carried our sorrows: yet we did esteem him stricken, smitten of God, and afflicted. But he was wounded for our transgressions, he was bruised for our iniquities: the chastisement of our peace was upon him; and with his stripes we are healed. All we like sheep have gone astray; we have turned every one to his own way; and the LORD hath laid on him the iniquity of us all."[28] And that is exactly what Jesus of Nazareth did with his life.[29]

The end of suffering sounds great, but not at the expense of justice. Suffering is only a small piece of the huge burden that evil leaves.[30] When a mother takes the life of her unborn child through surgical abortion, she avoids the pains of childbirth and leaves with only minor aches and pains after her procedure. Over the years, however, the fact that she took her child's life can haunt her, and then the real suffering begins. But the greater burden is not the suffering of a mother who feels bad about her action, it is the tragedy that the potential of an entire human life was lost in that brief moment of evil.[31] The mother can be taught to hush her conscience and sleep well, but the potential of her child is forever wasted. Suffering is no more than a small

piece of the real problem, and as a rule eliminating the
suffering does *not* eliminate the problem.[32]

Parenting in general requires a lot from us.[33] To
raise a family well, parents need to hold and carry their
children—sometimes quite literally. If our goal in life is
to end suffering by letting go, then childbirth and
parenting are less than ideal for sure. In fact, life itself
would be less than ideal. This is not empty
speculation—Buddhists, Hindus, and many others
around the world have as their highest goal the hope of
escaping the repetitious burden of life.

Billions around the world believe that life
obligates them to keep improving—even if it takes
thousands of rebirths—with the final goal of escaping
the sentence of birth into this world. That may seem
like an empty way to view life. And it is. A life robbed
of value cannot afford any real compassion.

Full of nothing?

Thich Nhat Hanh—as he likes to be known—is an
influential Buddhist monk considered by many to be
the greatest Zen Master of our time. He published an
article in 2012 on "the Fullness of Emptiness" in which
he discusses the object of Buddhism. The ultimate goal
of Buddhism is complete emptiness. That is not an
empty critique of Buddhist teachings, it is the religion's
stated objective.

Nhat Hanh suggests that all things in the universe "inter-are." His new word "inter-are" implies that the pieces of a system are dependent on one another in order to exist at all. In the absence of any piece, everything else would cease to exist. Nhat Hanh concludes that we are nothing but a composite of everything around us, and the person that we think we are is actually nothing but completely empty space.

Although it is true that a person's body depends on the elements of nature to exist, that fact does not somehow rob the body of its significance any more than the use of ink and paper for printing a book robs words of their meaning. Words have power, and people are much more than the bodies we have.[34] Most of us enjoy having our own space, but to claim that a person is nothing more than empty space is a serious misjudgment of reality. Furthermore, space is not a human invention, nor does it depend on us to exist.[35] The concept that the universe depends on us to exist is silly, and seems deeply arrogant. If humanity ceases to exist, space and the reality of our universe will not implode because of it—regardless of Nhat Hanh's opinions.

Hindu thought seems to contradict this Buddhist concept of emptiness at first glance, but a closer look reveals some surprising similarities. Hinduism holds that it is very important that we are one with the universe. The ability to see the larger context of reality and our place in it sounds nice, but the Hindu one-with-the-universe concept does not allow us to be an actual part of it. Hinduism teaches that we *are* the universe, and that the perception of individual people within the universe is a flawed and foolish concept. The sense of any distinct person in the human population is seen as a mere illusion to be scrubbed from our minds.

Hinduism leaves no place for individual life in the world because it, too, has accepted an incorrect view of the universe. In Hinduism the universe is infinite, but in natural science and good logic it is finite. The mass of the universe has been calculated by astrophysicists, and there is specific evidence to show that the mass of the universe is carefully balanced with its rate of expansion. But in a world where things have precise weights and values, clear logic also reveals the finite nature of the universe.

Hinduism teaches that each of us is actually everything because infinity divided by any number is still infinity. That concept, however, would work only in an artificial reality not in the real universe in which we exist. One ounce of gold has specific value; it is *not* the same as an infinite amount of gold.[36] That is reality.

So to recap what we just looked at, both Buddhism and Hinduism see an individual's life here as an illusion. Buddhism emphasizes emptiness, and Hinduism emphasizes fullness; but both deny the value of an individual's life. Buddhism tells us that we are to be empty space simply used by the laws of nature, and Hinduism tells us to embrace everything because we are one and the same as everything else in the universe.

One in five precious people currently living on earth—more than 1.7 billion—identify as either Hindu or Buddhist and have thus been led into empty philosophies with no lasting vision for their unique lives and no hope of real forgiveness.

Broke the mold

If you have ever had the pleasure of holding a newborn baby, you have good reason to appreciate the sacredness of a human life.[37] We know from science that no two people are actually identical. Even identical twins develop small changes in their genes, and through the course of their lives each becomes a very distinct individual.[38]

Marriage emphasizes this point well. When we take a spouse in marriage, we are saying loud and clear, "This person is the *one* for me." For anyone with a healthy sense of reality, the uniqueness of a person ought to command an extremely high value.[39]

The life that you are living right now has never had a duplicate, and it never will. During the 19th-century Industrial Revolution, new machines brought amazing efficiency to the production of goods in several countries. The ability to quickly duplicate products mechanically was the key. But we as humans are not duplicates run off a mechanical assembly line.[40]

A generic person does not exist in the natural world, and it would be wise to reflect on that reality for a good while. *There is no such thing as a generic human being. Each of us is a one-off masterwork.*

When the harshest storms sweep through our lives, the one thing that can never be replaced is a person.[41] Think about it.

Let's take a few minutes to look at some examples from Jewish history.

An awesome face

Abraham's wife, Sarah, hoped for many years to have a child, and when she finally conceived and gave birth, she was so old that it was against all odds. Abraham named the child Isaac, which means laughter. At that point Abraham and Sarah both knew that they should not be able to have this child, and to look at their son was to see the impossible made possible. Isaac was appreciated deeply and brought great joy to his family, particularly because his parents knew so well that he was impossible to reproduce and also impossible to place a value on.[42]

Both Isaac[43] and later his son Jacob also experienced some difficulty having children. Jacob's second wife Rachel told him, "Give me children, or else I die."[44] Jacob wanted Rachel to have children too, of course, but it was beyond his control. Like his grandfather, Abraham, Jacob had to learn a lot of patience in this area. And so it was that when Rachel finally did have a child, Jacob had a special depth of love toward him.

When Rachel's first son Joseph was 17, Jacob gave him a special coat. The coat consisted of many colorful pieces of material sewn together by Jacob's hand, and it provided an excellent symbol of Joseph's uniqueness in his dad's eyes. Joseph had several half-brothers, and they were not impressed by Joseph's special gift. They were jealous and angry that Joseph was honored in such a way, and they could not have good conversation with him because of it.[45]

One day Joseph had an unusual dream and shared it enthusiastically with his brothers. In the dream they were all working together to harvest stalks of grain, and when each of them had tied up his sheaf, Joseph's sheaf stood taller than those of his brothers. In Joseph's dream, all his brother's sheaves bowed in admiration toward his sheaf. Joseph believed the dream had some real meaning, and so the flames of hatred that his brothers had toward him were only fanned and intensified. They spoke to him defensively and mocked his words.[46]

Then Joseph had another dream. This time he dreamed that the sun, moon, and 11 stars bowed in respect to him. He was excited about it, and once again—probably against better judgment—shared the dream with his brothers, and then proceeded to tell his father. Jacob rebuked him. The dream implied that Joseph's parents and brothers would one day bow to him in admiration, and this suggestion seemed disrespectful to Jacob. But Joseph really believed that the dream meant something important. His brothers did not; they were livid.[47]

A few days later Joseph was asked to go check on his brothers. They were miles from home tending their father Jacob's sheep, and Joseph went to make sure all was well. Often in the past he had found them doing things that they did not want their father to know about. When the brothers finally saw Joseph coming out to them, they started discussing among themselves how they should deal with "this dreamer."[48]

Most of them literally wanted to kill him, but his oldest brother persuaded them to throw Joseph in a dry pit to divert their rage. It worked temporarily, but one of the other brothers was crafty enough to realize that there was a way to turn a *profit* on Joseph and keep their own hands clean at the same time. All they needed to do was sell him into slavery and tell their father he had died, and that would solve the problem—they would never have to see Joseph again.[49]

So his brothers sold Joseph as a slave for 20 pieces of silver and shipped him off. The slave traders took him across the Sinai Peninsula and retailed him in Egypt—about 240 miles from his family. But Joseph was not crushed by the injustice. He trusted in the God of his father and had a depth of wisdom and a bold spirit about him. His owner, Potiphar, grew to respect him deeply and allowed him to have many freedoms in the household.[50]

Joseph was doing very well in Egypt, but he soon found himself under attack again. Potiphar's wife began to admire Joseph inappropriately and secretly approached him with a proposition of infidelity toward her own husband. Joseph rejected her offers and told her that such a deed would be a betrayal of Potiphar's trust—and more importantly—"sin against God." She was persistent for many days, but Joseph would not abandon his integrity.[51]

One day Potiphar's wife found Joseph alone and took hold of his outer garment. But he pulled away from her and left it in her hands. She felt scorned and angry and decided to slander him. She called the other servants and told them that Joseph had approached her and left his garment only when she called for help. When Potiphar came home she rehearsed the same story to him. Potiphar was very upset with Joseph and had him put in prison for the alleged offense.[52]

So Joseph found himself in prison in Egypt. And, once again, he was able to trust the God of his father and to move forward with confidence—in prison. The prison keeper saw how well Joseph conducted himself and soon promoted Joseph to a position of authority among the prisoners. He spent over two years in prison, but he was not destroyed by it.[53]

One night the Pharaoh of Egypt had two similar dreams, and they bothered him. He wanted to understand why he had those dreams and what they implied, but none of his counselors could give him a clear answer. Then, suddenly, Joseph's name came up.

Pharaoh's head butler had met Joseph during a short stint in prison, and Joseph had helped him to understand one of his own dreams very well. The butler mentioned that Joseph was especially good at interpreting dreams, and Pharaoh called Joseph out of prison.[54]

When Joseph arrived, Pharaoh reminded him that he had a good reputation for interpreting dreams, and Joseph responded candidly, "It is not in me: God shall give Pharaoh an answer of peace."

In the first dream there were seven fat and healthy cattle that came out of the river and fed in a meadow, then seven very thin and ill cattle came up after them. The seven thin cattle ate the seven fat cattle and they were still just as thin and ill. Pharaoh woke, and when he fell asleep again, he had another dream. In the second dream there were seven good full ears of grain that came up on one stalk, and then there were seven withered, thin, and wind-beaten ears on another stalk. Then the thin ears devoured the full ears. And the Pharaoh woke again.[55]

Joseph's initial response to the dreams reflected the same wisdom that had motivated his father to stitch together a coat of many colors years earlier. Joseph said, "The dream of Pharaoh is one: God hath shewed Pharaoh what he is about to do." In other words, all the details of those dreams have one very specific application right now. Joseph went on to explain that the seven fat cattle and the seven full ears were illustrating seven years of great conditions to raise crops, and the seven thin cattle and the seven withered ears were illustrating seven years of drought to follow.[56]

He explained that the years of drought would consume the years of plenty just like the thin cattle and withered ears had eaten the others. Further, the dream was doubled to show the urgency and to confirm it. Joseph recommended finding competent people to organize stockpiles in Egypt during the good years. Pharaoh agreed and said to his attendants, "Can we find such a one as this is, a man in whom the Spirit of God is?" And thus Joseph was selected to lead that team.[57]

Joseph had been living the principle of Pharaoh's dreams for many years. He appreciated the benefits of his life deeply and was able to stockpile those benefits internally. He was not ruined when the hard times came but still enjoyed the old crops. He cut the stalks of grain closer to the ground to get every bit of straw that he could, and that's why his sheaf would stand taller than those of his brothers. He saw that the benefit of the harvest went deeper than most realized, and he gleaned more of the forgotten morsels.

But Joseph's level of appreciation was not simply a selfish ambition. He saw the goodness of his God toward all of us in the benefits of life. He realized that wasting those benefits was a general tragedy for everyone.[58] When Joseph's life seemed to crumble, he just kept his eyes on the goodness of his God. He believed that he was a part of his Master's work and felt blessed to fill that part—even if it was uncomfortable at times.

Joseph could embrace his time in slavery and prison because he believed that his true Master was bigger than those things and could work masterfully through them.[59] Joseph's greatest ambition was to be a part of his Master's work, and he was willing to take a back seat—at any point—to go along with him.

After embracing years of slavery and prison, Joseph understood the potential of his new position with phenomenal depth. He was in a position to serve millions, and that motivated him. Joseph had grown into an extraordinary leader by trusting the greatest of all masters. And so it began.

There were seven great years in Egypt, and Joseph worked hard to maximize the opportunities of those years and to preserve one-fifth of all the grain crops. They filled storehouses in many cities throughout the land. The bounty of the harvests in those years was overwhelming, but Joseph continued to stockpile. Then the good conditions came to an end.[60]

The drought began 20 years after Joseph's brothers had sold him into slavery. Those 20 pieces of silver that they profited were—no doubt—long spent or wasted, but the grief of Joseph's loss lived on in the heart of his father. And his brothers felt remorse for what they had done. As the drought set in, that remorse soon became unbearable.

The area affected by the drought was large and stretched far beyond Egypt to many other countries including Canaan—where Joseph was raised. News of the Egyptian storehouses spread quickly, and people from far and wide began flooding into Egypt to buy food. Joseph's brothers were among them.[61]

Joseph was managing the grain sales in Egypt and quickly recognized his brothers when they arrived, but—after 21 years of Egyptian culture—the brothers did not recognize Joseph. They all bowed to him with their faces to the ground, and he spoke roughly to them through an interpreter so that they would not recognize who he was. Joseph, remembering the dreams from 21 years earlier, accused his brothers of being spies.[62]

Suddenly Joseph's brothers found themselves in a very uncomfortable position and tried to free themselves from his accusation. They began to explain that they were all sons of one man, that they had lost one of their brothers, and that the youngest had stayed home with their father. Joseph then had them thrown in prison for three days.[63]

On the third day Joseph came and spoke to his brothers again through an interpreter. He told them that they would need to leave one of their brothers in prison until they returned to Egypt with their youngest brother. That was his requirement to verify that they were not spies. If they failed to comply, Joseph would not do any other business with them.[64]

Joseph's brothers began talking with one another about how they should have never sold their brother into slavery and how it displeased God. They did this without realizing that Joseph understood their language. Moved, Joseph slipped out of the room and wept for a while.[65]

When he returned Joseph took the second-oldest brother, Simeon—whose name means "he has heard"—and bound him in the sight of his brothers. The rest of the brothers were given food for their families and sent on their way back to Canaan. And so they left Simeon and returned to their father.[66]

Jacob was distraught when they told him that they had left Simeon behind and would need to take the youngest brother with them on their return to Egypt. The youngest brother—Benjamin—was the only child of Rachel beside Joseph, and she had lost her life in birthing him. Jacob could not bear the thought of losing him, and he told the other brothers that sending Benjamin to Egypt would not be an option.[67]

But the drought would not relent, and the food they got from Egypt was eaten up. The brothers tried to persuade their father to let Benjamin return with them, but he refused. Then Judah—the one who had suggested selling Joseph in the first place—reasoned with his father. He pledged his life to protect Benjamin and bring him back safely. Judah sealed it with a pledge: If he failed to return with Benjamin "then let me bear the blame for ever." So Jacob resigned his arguments and let Benjamin go with his brothers back to Egypt. They took the best gifts they could and extra money to buy grain.[68]

When they all arrived in Egypt, they were invited to Joseph's house. The invitation made them feel very uneasy, but they needed to comply. To their surprise they actually ate a nice meal there. For some reason Benjamin was given five times as much as any of his brothers, but it did not seem to bother any of them. They all just enjoyed the time together.[69]

After the meal Joseph told his steward to load up all the brothers' sacks with as much grain as they could carry and to put their money back in their sacks. Joseph instructed the steward to also place Joseph's silver cup in Benjamin's sack.[70]

Early in the morning the donkeys were loaded, and the brothers headed out of Egypt. But Joseph's steward went out quickly after them and stopped them as Joseph had instructed. He accused the brothers of stealing Joseph's silver cup, and they all offered to have their bags inspected. The steward opened each sack from oldest to youngest, and they were all horrified to see the cup in Benjamin's sack.[71]

The steward told all the other brothers to carry on to Canaan, and he would take Benjamin back to serve in Egypt. But none of the brothers would let that happen. So they all came back to Egypt with the steward and came into Joseph's house. When they saw Joseph all of them bowed to the ground in shame.[72]

Joseph reproved them. Judah spoke up to receive the brunt of the blame. He told Joseph that all the brothers should be servants in Egypt for what was done. Joseph responded, "God forbid that I should do so: but the man in whose hand the cup is found, he shall be my servant; and as for you, get you up in peace unto your father." Other than Benjamin, they were all given an official pardon. But then something wonderful happened.[73]

Judah walked up close to Joseph and began rehearsing this long complex story about what happened leading up to that day. He went on and on explaining all the precious details of his history. And in the end, Judah begged Joseph for the opportunity to take Benjamin's place, so that Benjamin could return to his father in Canaan. Judah could not bear to cause his father any more grief.[74]

Joseph had his answer. It was the answer he had hungered for above the riches of Egypt. His brother had a new heart, and authentic compassion by the very touch of God.

He hastily ordered all the Egyptian men to leave the room. Then Joseph began revealing himself to his brothers. He spoke in his native language and said, "I am Joseph; doth my father yet live?" His brothers just stood speechless, and Joseph asked them all to move in closer. Then he said, "I am Joseph your brother, whom ye sold into Egypt. Now therefore be not grieved, nor angry with yourselves, that ye sold me hither: for God did send me before you to preserve life."[75]

That was the greatest point of everything. The God of Jacob had worked mightily in and through the lives of Jacob's sons. That storm was past, and the calm was fragrant and deeply nourishing. Joseph spoke with each of his brothers and embraced them one by one. And after they wept together, his brothers began speaking with him.[76]

Within a few months Joseph's whole family moved to Egypt, and he was reunited with his father as well. There were still five years of drought remaining when Joseph revealed himself to his brothers, but there was no drought in the spirits of that family. The God of

Abraham, Isaac, and Jacob had continued to love people individually, and there was no mistaking it.[77]

Joseph was able to forgive his brothers so thoroughly because he focused his life on the Master of forgiveness. He saw forgiveness himself and knew how to practice it well. Logically Joseph had some authority to forgive his brothers for their wrongs against him, and he was given a sacred opportunity to do that face-to-face. Joseph's voice carried a certain power to heal their consciences unlike any other human voice, and his brothers could legitimately heal from those words of forgiveness spoken by the very mouth of Joseph.

Often life does not afford us such excellent opportunities to reconcile with others. But the point must be made that ignoring our wrongs does not make them any less real. If we are not sorry for our evils, how can they be repaired?[78]

Joseph privately accepted the actions of his brothers when they sold him into slavery and pleaded to his God on their behalf. They would rightfully stand dumbstruck in awe and wonder one day, that such prayers could be answered and that they could be recipients of such grace.[79] For years the storm had raged, and in the end what it swept away was only lies. What remained was deep—and real—and better than anything they had ever witnessed before.

When Joseph's brothers sold him into slavery, they hoped they could rid themselves of him. But their actions were evil, and those actions carried many very specific and severe consequences. Human nature likes to minimize and excuse failures in general, and that is especially true of moral failures.

Just as we could never replace a human life, so it is impossible to fully correct any of our evils without help. Joseph spoke to his brothers and openly forgave them, but they could never deserve his forgiveness and could never force it. Joseph could not correct the evil that his brothers had done, but he could personally forgive them on his end.

Joseph's brothers did wrong, and their actions hurt many people. The problem was real and deep. People want to let go of their evil deeds and live as if those deeds never happened, but denial does not change reality. Joseph's surprise reunion with his brothers illustrates well the reality of our forgotten evils.

Joseph's forgiveness was powerful and glorious, but it took stormy circumstances for his brothers to appreciate it. We will never appreciate the solution if we deny the problem. And it is often the harshest storms that reveal our true evils and the awesome face of real hope to conquer those evils.

CHAPTER 3:
Encountering the Person

There was a blizzard of glitter in the Walmart seasonal department, and we could not stock the little string lights fast enough. The overhead music was on a short rotation, and "kids from 1 to 92" was feeling a little old. It was winter break of 2001, and I was home from college working a second job in the evenings. Our Buffalo December had been unusually mild that year, so stepping outside to collect shopping carts from time to time was pretty refreshing—though 81 inches of snowfall at the end of the month turned out to be a bit more challenging for pushing carts.

There was one other reprieve from the glitter storm, and it was always very welcome in my world. The evergreen trees smelled fresh and authentic, and it was my job and pleasure to slip out into the cool air and wrap them for customers. People were usually friendly and excited about buying a live tree to decorate their home for the holidays. It was a very old and cherished tradition for most.

As I slid a certain tree into the mesh and spun it to cinch the branches down, the young lady buying the tree was chatting with her friend about her "first Christmas tree." I listened, curious. My parents had not done Christmas trees in our home, but I had assumed that most people in America were raised with them. So I asked her about it and found out she was Jewish. That was not what I expected to hear.

It threw me back for a second before I asked, "What do you believe about Jesus?" She replied very frankly, "Oh, I don't believe he's the Messiah." Then why was she buying a "Christmas tree?" I wondered. So I just went ahead and said it out loud. Her candid response exposed an empty goal of billions around the world. She said, "It's just a tradition."

And it is just a tradition. No one would be naïve enough to believe that wrapping wires along your gutters and throwing tinsel on a small rootless evergreen in your living room is reliable evidence of what you hold sacred. You might keep those traditions for any *number* of reasons.

Tradition is a means

But there is a real question that demands an answer. What is sacred to you?[1] When all the religious accessories are stripped away, what is left of your essential beliefs? Tradition is not the end. It was never meant to be the end or the goal of anything. Traditions are meant to remind us that there's something worth remembering. So if we have tradition without substance, all we have is an ineffective reminder of something supposedly more important—and lost.

People get lost in details all the time. And empty traditions are an engine of confusing details. Traditions are supposed to point us to things worth remembering, but many have the opposite effect.[2]

Good traditions are like trail markers left by responsible hikers to help us see all the key points in a natural region and how they relate to each other. The overwhelming majority of traditions, however, are not good ones—and the proof is in the pointlessness.[3] Empty traditions are like scads of litter scattered throughout the woods by irresponsible visitors that do nothing but clutter the path and make it harder to see the beauty of what matters.

That may seem like an attack on tradition, but it is not. The point here is that we need to keep our traditions meaningful lest they become nothing but a waste of precious time and energy. The sad reality is that people around the world are spinning their wheels to keep up with empty traditions and missing the greater opportunities of life. Tradition is a means. It is not an end.

Too much practice

There are roughly 80,000 public shrines throughout the great nation of Japan. The most iconic element of these are the torii—the shrine gateways. The torii are a well-known symbol around the world, generally consisting of two uprights and two crosspieces. In Shintoism the function of the torii is to mark a transition between the common and the sacred. When approaching a Shinto shrine, the moment that we pass through the torii, we would expect to leave the mundane and enter the realm of the divine. This ability to see beyond the temporary world and glimpse eternal things is a constant pursuit of many traditions around the world.[4]

One of the most important rituals within the grounds of a Shinto shrine is purification. Shintoism emphasizes that our spiritual impurities need to be cleansed before we can pray—another constant pursuit common to many traditions around the world.[5] At a Shinto shrine cold water is used in an attempt to wash away spiritual impurities. There is a water basin known as a temizuya and a ladle for scooping water.

The ladle is first held in the right hand to scoop water from the temizuya. Once the water is collected some is poured on the left hand, then using the left to hold the ladle, some is poured on the right hand. The ladle is then held with the right hand again, and water is poured into a cupped left hand. The water in the left hand is raised up to wet the participant's mouth and again water is poured on the left hand to cleanse it. Finally the remaining water is emptied from the ladle by raising it up and letting it run down the handle. After this process a visitor is considered cleansed to go pray at the main building.

Once at the main building of a shrine, it is recommended that visitors leave money before praying. Although no specific amount is required, 5 yen (roughly one US nickel) is a very common amount and implies good luck with relationships. After this coin is placed in the box, the visitor rings a bell, stands off to the side, bows twice, and—while holding the left hand slightly higher—claps twice. At this point the visitor is considered ready to pray. After praying, the visitor is to bow once more to complete the process.

Although these traditions have elements that seem to point visitors in the right direction spiritually, they are surprisingly empty by design. Followers of Shinto traditions do not expect to experience any real relationship with the deities they are pursuing.[6] All the tradition amounts to no more than mental conditioning and wishful thinking for good luck. Some more dedicated participants will take ceremonial public baths in extremely cold water to purify themselves at the start of a new year, but it is strictly ceremonial. They will openly admit that their traditions do not lead to anything specific. It is simply tradition for the sake of tradition and positive thinking.

There are 126 million individuals in Japan, and roughly 80% of these practice Shintoism. Tokyo's famous Meiji Shrine typically has over 3 million visitors within the first few days of the New Year, many of whom are hoping to experience good luck moving forward. But beyond luck there is no greater answer for their lives in Shintoism, and this is a profound tragedy. At a Shinto shrine you can purchase good luck charms and buy little boards to write wishes. And when you pass back through the torii to leave a shrine, the symbolism is unmistakable. You leave with nothing more than, perhaps, a wish for good luck.

That approach could seem adequate if there were nothing much to this life. But if life has serious value to it, wishful thinking and good luck charms are not enough. We should expect real answers for our real life outside the shrines and temples.[7] Life is not a trivial matter. It is not practice.

Sure as you are living

Solomon—one of the great leaders in Jewish history—was known for his amazing life insights. Early in his reign he prayed emphatically for wisdom, and he got it.[8] He saw right through things that needed discernment and was not one to role dice on serious matters.

One day two women were brought to Solomon for judgment. Both women had a reputation for loose morals, and both had recently given birth—just three days apart. The two women lived in the same house. On a certain night one of the women had rolled over on her child and suffocated him. When she woke up, she realized what had happened and quietly replaced the other woman's son with the dead son while the other slept. When the other woman woke, she saw the dead child with her, but realized that it was not her own son. No one else in the house had witnessed the event, so the two women just argued back and forth about the living child.[9]

After Solomon heard the case, he had a very strange but ingenious solution. He brought in a sword and said, "Divide the living child in two, and give half to the one, and half to the other." Then the real mother spoke out immediately, "O my lord, give her the living child, and in no wise slay it." The other woman was very neutral and diplomatic, and said "Let it be neither mine nor thine, but divide it." And Solomon had his answer. The true mother left with her whole living son.[10]

A woman who is indifferent about the life of a child does not show the marks of a labor with that child.

Similarly, a person who labors earnestly to see the face of reality cannot sit by passively while it is dispatched. It is not possible. If we really care enough to discover truth, we care too much to see it replaced with lifeless uncertainties on our watch.

Truth cannot be sliced up to please us all. It is certain and unbending. Before you get ahold of truth, it will get ahold of you.[11] And when it does get ahold of you, uncertainty will look cruel and vile in comparison.

A divine checkup

If God Himself could see right through your life and call you out on exactly where you are at, would you take it to heart? Any child can be taught to say nice things to others[12]—and children *should* be taught to do so—but to recognize life-threatening illnesses and know how to treat them requires time and intense training. We value highly trained doctors, and we are often willing to pay steep fees to talk with them about our health concerns;[13] but how do we value our spiritual health in comparison?

The greatest tools given to humanity for finding spiritual health objectively are our natural conscience and the Ten Commandments of Moses.[14] The conscience is the part of our mind that pieces together moral facts objectively, and it will not hesitate to find us guilty.[15] It is interesting to note that the word "conscience" literally means "with knowledge" or "with science." The beauty of the conscience is that it acts with mechanical precision inside of us—doing its own scientific research even without our permission. The conscience is an integral part of who we are, so we have good reason to take its conclusions seriously.

The conscience works in our lives to establish moral laws internally, but often we rationalize those laws to make them more convenient and palatable. This can lead to an artificial sense of uncertainty. The conscience is very objective, but human nature creates ways to excuse it, fueling a repetitive cycle of law and lawlessness.[16]

The Shinto shrines are marked with a torii symbol on most local maps, symbolizing this constant cycle of standards inside the shrines and profanity outside of them. In Shintoism there is a waxing and waning of standards that leads to nowhere in particular, and the torii symbolizes that well. In the same way the Buddhist temples are marked with a swastika, or "hooked cross" as it is known in many languages—a symbol cherished by most Jains and Hindus as well. In Buddhism the swastika pictures the footprints of Buddha, and a never-ending cycle of life and death.

The word swastika means conducive to well-being. It was used notoriously by Adolph Hitler during WWII to symbolize the struggle of Aryans to thrive at any cost, but the concept fundamentally belongs to religions that emphasize our happiness. If happiness or the end of our suffering is the main goal of a religion, then nothing—including cutting the cords of our conscience—is too high a cost to obtain that goal.[17] It is a slippery and deceptive path. If we are going to gain some good initial traction and make real spiritual headway in this life, there is no substitute for firmly anchored laws and a healthy conscience.

The Ten Commandments were given to Moses to help us avoid cycles of law and excuse, and he said these laws were engraved in stone "written with the finger of God."[18] The power of these sacred words evidences their authority. As the Book of Hebrews puts it, "For the word of God is quick, and powerful, and sharper than any twoedged sword, piercing even to the dividing asunder of soul and spirit, and of the joints and marrow, and is a discerner of the thoughts and intents of the heart."[19] Our own conscience will readily confirm these commandments as if it shares a common origin with them, and this is evidence of a deeper sort—that both conscience and commandments were given to us by God.[20]

The Ten Commandments are simple laws that are easy to agree with. The laws are so intuitive for our natural conscience that similar laws can be found around the world, in traditions such as Confucianism. The truth of them is so cutting that even those who oppose moral standards and religious traditions of all sorts still want to believe that they obey the ninth commandment for instance—that they are honest people.

One of the great advantages of the Ten Commandments is that they are clear and precise. The exact words used in the Ten Commandments are very direct and to the point. In English the word "Thou" begins 8 of the 10 commandments, and it is a second person singular pronoun—meaning this is addressed to "you" as an individual.[21] All through the passage we see an emphasis on the individual, and how the God of Abraham does not believe in the existence of a generic person. Each person has an opportunity—and a mandate, in fact—to have a personal encounter and relationship with the God of Abraham.[22]

Is it possible that the same God who keeps track of every atom in the galaxy Andromeda cares profoundly about the exact details of each person on this planet? That is the God of Abraham, Isaac, and Jacob, and he does care intensely for you as an individual—unlike anyone else ever could.[23] It is these amazing Ten Commandments that bring us face to face with the reality of our own history and into the presence of another Person who can make all things new.[24]

The God of Abraham does not believe in fair-weather friendships. He teaches us that good friends should love at all times, and this is especially important when life gets stormy.[25] A real friend still cares when it is least convenient and when matters go far below the surface. That kind of friend will take the time to understand our situation in depth and get involved with it on a deep and personal level.

A real friend knows how to carry you when you cannot carry yourself.[26] The God of Abraham calls people out into a new life with him. He sees the reality of potential in our lives that others could not imagine and longs to work with us to help us realize our full potential.[27] The Ten Commandments open an important door, working as "our schoolmaster" to lead us into this extraordinary relationship.[28]

An ambitious stranger

A certain woman who lived in Samaria in the first half of the 1st century discovered this principle in a big way.[29] She had worked hard at her relationships for many years, but there was a theme of emptiness to all of them. Her life was marked by one broken marriage after another, and she was starting yet another relationship hoping that it would go better. She believed in positive thinking and thought this one would be different.

The woman was also very proud of her heritage. The Samaritans were descendants of Abraham who had been mixed with invading Assyrians for over 700 years at that point, and they had developed their own traditions separate from other Jews. Samaritans believed that their land—in the middle of Israel—was the original and true land of Abraham. They worshipped on Mount Gerizim where Moses himself had once instructed God's people to worship, and they believed that they were able to get the benefits of Moses' God in their own lives.

Hoping for some better luck in her relationships, the woman walked out of the city of Sychar where she was staying at the time and visited a very holy place in her religion. It was only a short distance outside the city limits, but it was a big destination for her. She went out to the well of Jacob—the same well that the grandson of Abraham had used so many generations before.

The water she drew from it was like holy water that could ease her conscience somewhat. That water allowed her to connect with her ancestors and to share their faith in a sense. She knew that it was just ordinary water in that well, recycled by many rainfalls over the centuries, but it gave her a shadow of something to cling to.

She had come out to visit that comforting place many times over the years and knew it well. She knew how deeply she would have to lower a pot into that pit and how long her cord would need to be in order to pull the precious water out of its mouth. The ladies of the city would often go to gather water in the evenings, and she knew how to avoid that crowd. She planned her visit close to noon—in the heat of the day—but she was not alone there this time.

While approaching the historic site she noticed a man resting on top of her cherished relic. His choice of seat may have seemed a bit uncultured to her; and as she walked up, the undignified stranger spoke right out to her. He was clearly a Jewish man with grit enough to ask a Samaritan woman for a favor while sitting on her country's sacred relic. He said rather bluntly, "Give me to drink."

The woman's solemn tradition at Jacob's well was quickly becoming a shipwreck that day. This was very awkward. The Jews avoided the Samaritans whom they deemed an inferior race, and the wedge was driven very deep over the course of seven centuries. What kind of Jewish man would walk into Samaria and expect a favor from a woman of that culture? It was incredibly puzzling to her. She responded by asking how he could ignore such cultural barricades and reminded him that "the Jews have no dealings with the Samaritans."

The man was unfazed. He told her that if she knew the gift of God and who it was who said, "Give me to drink," she would have asked him for water. He told the Samaritan that he had "living water" to offer her—as if it was better than water from that sacred well, better than what she could offer him.

At this point she was bristling in pride and began to pick apart his lofty claim. For one thing the man sitting on the well seemed to have nothing to draw water with, and she could not imagine a more sacred source than this legendary place. She said, "Sir, thou hast nothing to draw with, and the well is deep: from whence then hast thou that living water? Art thou greater than our father Jacob, which gave us the well, and drank thereof himself, and his children, and his cattle?"

She was right to honor the memory of Abraham's grandson and her roots common with the Jews; but what she said was true—the well was deep and it was dark down there even at high noon.

There was something more sacred to all of this because pictured in that well was the soul of this Samaritan woman. How many times had she drawn from that relic? And never had it cleansed more than the surface. It was like her Shinto temizuya that wet the surface of her hands and lips, but deep inside she lived in darkness year-round. That well within her was deep and dark, and beyond the reach of clear daylight or personal contact—until now.

The man replied with a simple truth, and it was undeniable. He said that the water in Jacob's well was not an enduring solution, and those who drink it would inevitably "thirst again." It was an obvious statement of fact, but it was also a reality check about the limits of tradition. No amount of tradition can substitute for real

spiritual health. Tradition is powerless to purify our
wrongs, and it is powerless to move us forward. His
simple statement was so natural and intuitive that it
quickly disarmed her.

This "living water" that he recommended was
unlike anything she had experienced before. He said that
any person who drinks this living water would "never
thirst," and he continued, "the water that I shall give him
shall be in him a well of water springing up into
everlasting life."

What a contrast! Rather than straining to reach
into a dark pit of regrets, there was a power available to
bring them up above ground and to celebrate a great
victory over all those regrets. The man was offering a life
beyond shame and cover-ups, and the Samaritan woman
had been through enough of that sort of thing to sense it
and to seize on the offer swiftly.

By the time he finished his sentence she was no
longer defensive about her culture and traditions. The
woman was broken enough to allow the truth into her
shell and to respond to it pretty candidly. She had little
to lose, and she knew for sure that something was
missing in her life. So without really knowing what she
was asking for, she went ahead and took him up on his
offer saying, "Sir, give me this water, that I thirst not,
neither come hither to draw."

Then the Jewish man carried a lamp—called the
Ten Commandments of Moses—into her soul and lit a

clear path to that living water she craved.[30] He said to her, "Go, call thy husband, and come hither." The command was precise and simple and sliced through many complex layers of veneer in her life.

The marital status of this Samaritan was a pungent embarrassment and a topic she hoped to dodge—nervously responding, "I have no husband." But her guarded words were more deadly accurate than she knew, and those words were about to echo sharply through the voids of her soul.

The Jew was insightful and quick. He responded, "Thou hast well said, I have no husband: For thou hast had five husbands; and he whom thou now hast is not thy husband: in that saidst thou truly." What she said was very true. In all her years she had never been honest enough to give her life to another person sincerely. Her promises were forever divided and unstable.

There was no man or friend to call her own on that day, not anyone, and that was a biting fact of her reality. She had many fleeting affairs but little foundation in any relationship, and her life overall was no more than a rough patchwork of tattered rags to show for it. There was no one holding her house together—in any sense.

How could she deny the fact? Much of her life had just been laid bare in that one magnificent sentence.

But where could she go to make things right? Her
ancestors had worshipped on Mount Gerizim for
centuries, and the Jews did not want her at the temple in
Jerusalem. If the Samaritan traditions were not enough
to meet the needs of her soul, where else could she go?
She was a Samaritan by birth, and there was nothing she
could do to change that. There was no place for her at
the temple in Jerusalem.

    She denied nothing. Rather she confirmed the
wisdom of this outspoken Jew and the reality of her
impossible position—saying, "Sir, I perceive that thou
art a prophet. Our fathers worshipped in this mountain;
and ye say, that in Jerusalem is the place where men
ought to worship." Her life had become a prison of her
own making, her long record of empty promises had left
her with nothing to believe in, and her old birthright
provided no good way for her to live healthy and free
again. If there was something better in Jerusalem, the
cold fact of the matter was, she was not welcome there.

    Her complex path of many years had reached its
greatest climax and conclusion when she hit this wall.
She could not repair the trail of wreckage, and she could
not replace the years she had lost. What was done was
final, and what needed to happen was bigger than
anything she could do. She was certain of that.

    The Samaritan's bold candor was refreshing, and
the Jew was moved with potent compassion in response
to it. He demanded hope for her life, saying, "Woman,

believe me, the hour cometh, when ye shall neither in this mountain, nor yet at Jerusalem, worship the Father. Ye worship ye know not what: we know what we worship: for salvation is of the Jews." The Jew's compassion was tenacious—demanding her confidence and providing clear hope for her future. He spoke of "the Father" whom she could still know and of a personal "salvation" for a broken life.

But the Jew was also right about what she did not know. Her traditions were very truly no more than wishful thinking that helped her to forget her iniquity from time to time, but they offered no solution for it. The wrongs she had covered would never decompose well either, and her life was littered with them. She had many traditions designed to mask recurring problems, and those soothing traditions became addictive and religious over time. Her traditions had only added to her evils by stirring them into a thick and colorful broth of cheap fillers. The goal was blissful ignorance, and it worked pretty well for a while. But there was death in the pot, and she knew it.

That wonderful word "salvation" was unlike anything the Samaritan traditions had to offer. The word offered hope that a person could be salvaged. The word meant that a broken individual like her could be redeemed by active compassion rather than being consumed by tradition or emptiness. The Jew spoke of "the Father" who was worthy of all worship and guaranteed that she too could have a part in that worship. But how would it ever be possible for her to move forward respectably? How could that happen in the real world?

The Jew continued, "But the hour cometh, and now is, when the true worshippers shall worship the Father in spirit and in truth: for the Father seeketh such to worship him. God is a Spirit: and they that worship him must worship him in spirit and in truth." Twice more he had spoken of "the Father." He told her of true worshippers who—at the exact moment of that conversation—could worship right from their spirit with perfect honesty and without any pretense at all.

The Samaritan had lived through enough pretense and deception to know how ugly and regrettable that way is. Her reality was ugly and regrettable, and she was ready to call it what it was—a living nightmare of her own making. At some point the circus of pretense and deception must grind to a halt, and the truth must conquer all. She understood this terrifying reality and had courage enough to face it on the right side of the grave.

When the Jew spoke of the Father who is actively seeking individuals for a higher purpose, the Samaritan recalled prophecies about a man who would come into the world and change lives forever. He had been called "the Messiah" in Daniel's prophecies,[31] and his Greek title "the Christ" was also familiar to her. The sacrifices that took place throughout Jewish history all foretold of the need for this crucial man's life and work.[32] He would solve fundamental problems that no one else could, and—in a very personal way—would crush the most complex evils.

The Samaritan had come to a point in her life where she could really appreciate the Messiah's work. And she thirsted for it, saying, "I know that Messias cometh, which is called Christ: when he is come, he will tell us all things." The prophecies had passed through many generations, cultures, and languages, but the substance of that truth was something she knew for certain. Her conscience thirsted for the saving work of Christ, and the Spirit of God had taken the Ten Commandments like a burning lamp into her spirit and left her with no grain of hesitation about it.[33]

Her life had become yet another case-in-point affirming that the Messiah must come. She had known of the prophecies by word of mouth for many years, but now she knew the certainty of them by the shriek of her own conscience. She accepted the truth even though it ravaged her, and in turn the Jew disclosed his plan to be ravaged for her redemption. He revealed himself as the very Messiah—anticipated for 60 generations of human history—saying, "I that speak unto thee am he."

The Jew was none other than Jesus of Nazareth. His name means "salvation" and it can be seen throughout the Hebrew Bible[34]—he came to save his people from their sins.[35] He spoke of that salvation nearly 20 centuries ago when he met the Samaritan at Jacob's well, and his life mission is still the most crucial topic for every person alive today. The Samaritan had discovered a friend who understood her better than she understood herself, and she discovered a compassion that was real and competent. She believed that this Jew could resolve her complex evils and change the nature of her sick heart.

As Jesus was making the statement about his identity, several other Jewish men who had been traveling with him returned from their errand to buy food in the city. They saw him conversing with the woman and were surprised to see it. But what they saw next was especially good.

The Samaritan abandoned her precious water pot and quickly headed back toward Sychar. It was an act of obedience and worship. The Jew had only asked her to do one thing in order to receive that living water for her soul, and to the best of her ability she would do that—she would go and call her husband. The Messiah had called her out, and she went to call out all that she had committed her life to and to bring it to the One who is worthy of more. For years she had tried to impress the men in her life and to win them to herself. And on this day she scrapped those social gains most gladly.

She came through the city of Sychar and spoke out to the men she knew there. With no reservation at all she called out to them, saying, "Come, see a man, which told me all things that ever I did: is not this the Christ?" She was over it. Her days of crafty social strategy and airtight denial had come to a close. The Jew understood her too well to be less than the Messiah, and she appreciated the ravaging truth of his message deeply.

Jesus was also refreshed by her bold appreciation, and within a short time she had led a crowd of men back to Jacob's well to hear him some more. When they heard the words of this man from Nazareth, they knew as well. Many of them testified, "[W]e have heard him ourselves, and know that this is indeed the Christ, the Saviour of the world."

What is it about Jesus of Nazareth that impacts some people so deeply and powerfully? Not everyone who met Jesus of Nazareth was so convinced. In fact, many people despised him and many still do. Most of the religious leaders in Judea were not happy with Jesus at all. He was traveling away from them back toward Galilee when he passed through Samaria and talked with the woman at Jacob's well that day. He cares more for us than we care for ourselves. That is ambitious!

Rugged and real

That Samaritan and many others would find an extraordinary relationship in Jesus of Nazareth, but it is the Ten Commandments of Moses that opens the door to that relationship. And that Law can seem very offensive. We can appreciate a heart surgeon who tells us that we have serious blockage and require a bypass surgery, but more often than not we erupt inside if anyone dares to imply that there may be moral impurities in our heart. We all know that there is plenty of evidence of evil in the world, but who wants to accept the blame for it?

It is completely humiliating to think that you are not good person at heart—that you are fundamentally impure by nature. But that is exactly what we learn from the Ten Commandments of Moses, and that is exactly what we learn from the work of the Messiah. People who have made a train wreck of their lives tend to be in a better position to be honest about this, yet some of the most successful figures in history have also faced that same terrifying reality with courage.

Jesus of Nazareth would often befriend those in town with the worst reputations, and it really irritated many of the religious folks.[36] One day when they were busy slandering him for it, he clarified something very important. He said, "They that are whole have no need of the physician, but they that are sick: I came not to call the righteous, but sinners to repentance."[37]

That is the mission statement that Jesus of Nazareth openly claimed—he came to call sinners to repentance. People who are good at heart before salvation have no use for the Messiah. They did not have use for the Messiah when Jesus of Nazareth walked the streets of Jerusalem, and they will not have use for a real Messiah any time soon. No real Messiah could ever help them because they do not qualify for his help. They refuse to qualify.[38]

Many like to associate with Judaism and Christianity, but few are willing to really embrace the Messiah's work.[39] The Muslims also recognize Jesus of Nazareth as a messiah, but they see his crucifixion as no more than an unfortunate miscarriage of justice. Like most followers of Atheism, Agnosticism, Eastern Mysticism, Judaism, and popular Christianity, the Muslims also consider themselves to be fundamentally good. This would exempt them from the Messiah's work. If they are not sick, they do not need a physician. For this reason, Islamic authorities view the identity and work of a messiah as fairly trivial.

The real question is not "Are you are a sinner?" but rather "Do you bear true witness to that fact and care to resolve it?" Looking good is an art that sly folks have been mastering for ages.[40] Anyone can claim that he or she is a good person, but that does not make it a fact.[41] A person can even have a long record of criminal activity and yet provide many reasons to explain why what they did was right and best. And many convicts will do just that. The most common path, however, is simply to deny that it ever happened at all, and—in the eyes of God—such denial is just as incredible for the polished religious person as it is for the most notorious convict.[42]

The truth must conquer all regardless of what we do with it on this side of the grave. The best thing that any one of us can do in this life is simply to be honest about our need for the Messiah and to recognize his value. The less you value being real with yourself and with God, the less you will value the Messiah. It really is that simple.

If we lack a love for the Messiah, it is because we have failed to be real with ourselves and with God.[43] All of us have much for which we need to be forgiven. So if we have never been forgiven of much, it is through no one's fault but our own; and it is assuredly to our own ruin.

Forgiveness is available for all who will seek it. Jesus of Nazareth made this very clear through his ministry, but it was common knowledge long before the 1st century. The prophet Isaiah wrote, "Come now, and let us reason together, saith the LORD: though your sins be as scarlet, they shall be as white as snow; though they be red like crimson, they shall be as wool."[44] We can be forgiven of much; but we must "come" to experience that forgiveness, or we will miss the opportunity.

The Samaritan at Jacob's well was willing to ask for that living water Jesus offered her, and she was eager to go back to Sychar and point every man she could to the source of help she found in the Messiah. Many others also saw a great need for the Messiah and valued him above all else. John the Baptist was a powerful prophet who preached about the Messiah in the barren wilderness of Judea, and many people went out of their way to hear him—knowing that they needed spiritual help.[45] Like his message, John was rugged and real.

A matchless treasure

Another great example of those who went out of their way to value the Messiah's work was a lady who lived a few miles outside of Jerusalem in the town of Bethany. Mary lived with her sister Martha and her brother Lazarus.[46] They all considered Jesus of Nazareth a dear friend, and he would visit their house from time to time.

One day when Jesus came to visit at the house in Bethany, it was abuzz with guests. Martha was stressed with the task of hosting such a crowd, but Mary just sat calmly on the floor and listened to Jesus teach. Martha felt irritated that her sister would just sit there while so many guests needed to be served and entertained, but it did not bother Jesus at all. In fact, he made an example of Mary and encouraged Martha to learn from her. He said, "Martha, Martha, thou art

careful and troubled about many things: But one thing
is needful: and Mary hath chosen that good part, which
shall not be taken away from her."[47]

Mary knew that she needed a Messiah, and his
work was very valuable to her. The name Mary actually
means "bitter,"[48] and implies that her parents had long
sought for a Messiah who could make her spiritually
pure. Mary had lived under that cloud for many years
and knew by her own conscience how vital the Messiah
would be for her, but Martha was missing it—distracted
by a flurry of details when the Messiah she so needed
came to her own house.

Through patient attention to his words and
actions, Mary of Bethany became thoroughly convinced
that Jesus of Nazareth was the prophesied Messiah.
Like the Samaritan who met him at Jacob's well, Mary
was deeply convinced of this by her own conscience to
the point she would boldly express her depth of
gratitude very publicly. She did something that was
absolutely brazen and yet surprisingly proper for the
occasion.

On that occasion, Jesus was again a dinner
guest at a home in Bethany. Jesus was sitting with
friends at the table. Martha was busy helping to serve
the meal again as usual. Mary entered the room and
walked up behind Jesus. She took a special container of
fragrant oil called spikenard and broke it above him so

that it soaked his back and feet where he was sitting on the floor.[49]

The oil was from spikenard plants harvested at high altitudes in the Himalayan Mountains. The underground stems of these rare plants are crushed and distilled to isolate the highly fragrant essential oil. The precious ointment would arrive in Israel only after being slowly and carefully transported over 3,000 miles. It was very expensive; 24 drops of the oil cost a day's labor, but it was potent, and each of those drops could go a long way. Mary brought a "pound" of the spikenard oil—a Roman *litra* of it—over 12 fluid ounces. What Mary did would be like pouring a large glass full of pure spikenard onto Jesus of Nazareth. It was worth a year's wages at 72 hours per week for most.

The smell was warm, woody, sweet, and organic with spicy tones. The fragrance was so rich and immersive that every skeptic in the room knew exactly what she had poured out, and they criticized her for it. She could have fed thousands of people with the proceeds of selling that pure spikenard she poured out. It seemed so wasteful to use so much in this way. But Mary was there to worship. She was not concerned with the opinions of those who were missing the opportunity. The Messiah is worth more than all else to a thirsty soul, and Mary was not going to miss her best moment to express that truth to the world.

Mary then crouched down behind where Jesus of Nazareth was seated on the ground and did something even more brazen and authentic. She brought her head down and anointed Jesus' feet with the pure spikenard—wiping it on his feet using her own hair as a cloth. She knew exactly what she was doing, but much more importantly she saw what her God was doing and was ravished by the beauty of it. Those feet had literally come for her and brought a glorious solution for her guilty soul. That same week Jesus would go to be crucified, and Mary was prophetically anointing his body for burial. She knew there would never be another treasure like that divine body.

Forever lost

Judas Iscariot—one of Jesus' closest followers—was also there when Mary anointed Jesus' feet. Judas was not moved much by Mary's act of worship. Within only a few hours of that event he had planned to betray his friend. After more than three years of close personal mentorship with Jesus of Nazareth, Judas Iscariot visited the chief priests and agreed to work with them to set up a quiet arrest in exchange for 30 pieces of silver.[50]

For years Judas Iscariot had spent many hours every day right beside the Messiah. They shared many meals and memories together, but Judas had never appreciated the real value of the Messiah's presence.

And he missed the crucial opportunity of his life in exchange for 30 cold little pieces of metal. It was a close encounter, but—for him—a tragically wasted one. His best opportunity was forever lost.

CHAPTER 4:
An Amazing Reality

Life is an amazing treasure that we can appreciate. All the many details that must come together to make a life possible are important, but what *happens* during that life is even more important. It is wonderful to hold a newborn and see a fresh little person separate from his or her mother. A newborn is not a simple extension of parents, but a new, wholly unique human being altogether.[1] And that person's experiences can come together for something much greater and more enduring than that person alone.[2]

A living person is not a simple mechanical body.[3] We have living potential—both for better and for worse. Like beavers in a stream, we do not need to simply go with the flow. We can bring down the mighty plants around us and *change* the flow and the landscape as we see fit. And, of course, our human potential far exceeds that of beavers in a stream. It is both a huge privilege and a huge liability.

The great advances we have made in technology recently are a great illustration of this. What other generations once thought impossible is now standard procedure on many fronts of life. We can do things with technology that are nearly miraculous, but along with those benefits there is some pretty nasty potential as well. Our phones, for instance, can run all kinds of useful apps; but they might also eat the most sacred minutes of your life if not kept in check.[4] And along with improved medicine comes some more advanced biological weapons designed to maximize the loss of human life and decrease world population.

All is not well in our world, by any means, but life is a great opportunity to learn what it means to be truly well and free. True freedom is a wonderful thing— and it is possible.[5] Yet the average person will never experience it, simply because too many settle for much less than real freedom.

When Jesus of Nazareth brought freedom for the Jews near Jerusalem, they told him they were "never in bondage."[6] They preferred to live in bondage rather than to admit that they were in bondage and embrace the freedom Jesus offered. There is an eternal principle that applied to those Jews just as well as it applies to us today. Jesus explained, "Whosoever committeth sin is the servant of sin."[7] You cannot live free if you are living in sin. It is impossible. The liar is chained to his lies, no matter how sweet they may seem.

Of all the potential that is found in human lives, the most amazing and enduring potential is the ability to know why we are here and how to truly live on that target for our lives.[8] This is possible, however, only if we deal with the reality of our sins. And—yes—sins do happen. A marksman cannot improve his aim if he ignores his misses; and we cannot get on target for our lives if we ignore our wrongs.

The power of technology is in the details. One glitch in a powerful computer can render it temporarily useless. When things are in order they have a certain power that would not be possible aside from such order.[9] This principle is often referred to as "emergence." We see this principle in physical systems like computers and cars, but it applies more generally to our personal potential as well.

Sin versus your potential

Hitting our real potential requires a well-ordered life.[10] Sin is a glitch in our life, but it is much more than that. Sin is defined as "the transgression of the law."[11] To transgress the law means that we step over and beyond the law. It is like trespassing on private property, and only rarely does it happen by accident. Even if we are completely ignorant of the Ten Commandments, our own natural conscience will leave us with zero excuse more often than not.[12] As a rule, sin is a purposeful decision to waste the immense gift of living potential in exchange for temporary things.[13] Like throwing your baby in the trash to go and catch a date, sin is more than a mere glitch—it is vile.

In our modern culture sin has become the object of much mockery, and most who mock it fail entirely to see the real and deadly nature of it.[14] Sin is not a joke, and it is not a matter of opinion. Sin is real and vile. Playing with sin is like playing Russian roulette with a partially loaded handgun—doing so will, in time, thoroughly destroy your potential.[15] And unlike Russian roulette sin comes with a bleak and certain promise. This is not what any one of us likes to hear, but it is reality, and the sooner we come to terms with this reality, the better. The wages of sin is death, and we can count on it.[16]

Knowing that death is more certain than taxes is a constant reminder of what sin does to our potential.[17] Sin destroys life. And—unlike taxes—death is impossible to cheat for long. The Book of Romans teaches that the universal influence of death in our world is actually direct evidence of our own deep and persistent sin nature. It says, "Wherefore, as by one man sin entered into the world, and death by sin; and so death passed upon all men, for that all have sinned."[18]

The fact that natural death is the inevitable end of natural processes in our current world reminds us that we humans have a big fundamental problem. It traces all the way back to the first generation and a promise of God. Adam was given a promise that he could freely eat of all the trees in the Garden of Eden except for one, and if he decided to eat from that one forbidden tree he had another promise. God promised, "in the day that thou eatest thereof thou shalt surely die."[19] Adam did eat from that one forbidden tree and he died that day just as God had promised. His body continued on for a while as an empty shell, but he was truly dead. His spirit died on that day, and his nature began to decay.

The generations that followed were all spiritually stillborn because of Adam's decision.[20] This sequence of events helps us to see the scope of Adam's choice. We often have a very small concept of what sin does, but seeing the entire earth's population affected by this man's decision is very sobering. If Adam's body had died that day, we would not be able to appreciate the scope of all that his sin affected. We would never have been born at all.

We have been given a great opportunity to study the events of human history and to gain some perspective on the scope of a man's sin. All of those born throughout our history were part of Adam's potential, and—given the vast potential of genetic recombination—they are only a small tip of the iceberg. All the suffering and evils that have compounded over the last several millennia are also part of that crippled potential. Sin has a huge ripple effect that is easy to forget about but still very real.

Even skeptics like Charles Darwin believe that human life must be traced back to a single human couple; and if that couple had destroyed their potential, we may not exist today. It is simple logic. Our life affects many others for better or for worse.[21] In a world of billions, we are prone to downplay our potential, but each one of us can have an effect on the world very much like the first man—Adam.

This is both inspiring and intimidating. We see that we can make a great difference, but there are many ways to go wrong in this life.[22] And when we miss the target others will often take a hit. Whether we are actively against others or simply failing to do what we should, missing the mark will hurt others around us. We are each meant to be a key part of a much bigger work. That is the great beauty and liability of this life. No person is an island in this world.[23]

Loss of potential can be just as deadly as murder. Many times a married couple cannot have children for medical reasons, but there are also many couples who would rather accumulate assets than have children. When a couple decides to place assets above children, there are long-term consequences that can directly affect hundreds of generations that follow. There is no set rule for when a couple should try to have children, but the point here is that a loss of potential can be very subtle and deadly serious.

A slight change in this illustration will make the point more vivid. Imagine instead a man who coveted his neighbor's assets and became so envious that he murdered his neighbor. We all tend to gasp at such obvious evil, and the man would rightly deserve to be condemned for such a crime. But the root evil was not murder, it was greed, which led to hateful envy. The last of the Ten Commandments is "Thou shalt not covet," and it is no less vital than the Sixth Commandment, "Thou shalt not kill." When the pursuit of assets begins to eat us up, we are wasting our real potential and are quite guilty in the eyes of God.[24] Sin will always erode our potential

The center of freedom

It is way too easy to get consumed with racking up assets and miss the whole point of life. Net worth assumes that you are going to be removed, and it has little to do with our actual worth. In fact, when Moses received the Ten Commandments it was during the Jewish Exodus from Egypt,[25] and the whole nation was illustrating the principle that people are more precious than possessions by their exodus. When God gave Moses the commandments, he first identified himself saying, "I am the LORD thy God, which have brought thee out of the land of Egypt, out of the house of bondage."[26]

Before God led them out, the Jews had become slaves in Egypt,[27] and in their slavery they were illustrating for us the bondage that comes with living for assets. Egypt had multiple cities filled with treasure,[28] and the whole nation was all about assets. We can easily get drawn into such lifeless greed, but the God of Abraham desires to pull us out of it. He is never impressed by our net value, but he invests much in our actual value.[29] He sees us each as a person, created in his own image,[30] and invests himself in us like none other.

We see this love of God in the First Commandment, when he said, "Thou shalt have no other gods before me."[31] Remember that he had just identified himself as "the LORD thy God." This means that while he is Jehovah—completely self-existent—he also committed himself willingly to the Jews. He said, "thy God," revealing that he was given to the Jews in a special way. The First Commandment also emphasizes this point when it uses the word "have." Again it says, "Thou shalt have no other gods before me." We see that the Jews can *have* Jehovah because he offers himself to them willingly.

If we give ourselves to something less than God, it is a guaranteed waste of our potential; and whatever else it is that we give ourselves to, we will not have it for long—guaranteed.[32] It makes perfect sense to keep the main point the one that we live for, but how do we really do that? People do not hold us accountable for this, yet it is absolutely essential for reaching our potential. And if we miss this, we miss the point of everything.

The Second Commandment gives us some practical guidance on this. We are commanded not to make any image to represent God. He is not our creation, we are his. This commandment is much more detailed than the first. It says, "Thou shalt not make unto thee any graven image, or any likeness of any thing that is in heaven above, or that is in the earth beneath, or that is in the water under the earth: Thou shalt not bow down thyself to them, nor serve them: for I the LORD thy God am a jealous God, visiting the iniquity of the fathers upon the children unto the third and fourth generation of them that hate me; And shewing mercy unto thousands of them that love me, and keep my commandments."[33]

We are helping no one when we try to replace the God of Abraham with relics and traditions. He is not an item for us to use. We were made by him, and we have no business trying to fit him into some box of human invention. When we use some image to stand in for God, we are proving that we do not care to know him personally. It is actually hateful toward him and a very dead way for us to exist.[34] This kind of lifeless religion can pass through many generations like a dirty habit, but it is much more vile than most. It is properly referred to as idolatry.

Idolatry takes many forms. Whether it is the emperor Constantine using a good luck symbol to advance the Roman agenda through violent combat or the lawless versions of grace embraced by modern "Christian" movements,[35] idolatry is hatred toward God. In order to love God, we must care about who he actually is.[36] And if we care about knowing the God of Abraham, we have to take his words to heart.[37] If we disregard his words and laws, we do not love him.

Playing around with the name of God is not a laughing matter. When we try to use God's reputation for personal advantage, he knows all about our games, and it is vile in his sight. The Third Commandment focuses on this point. It says, "Thou shalt not take the name of the LORD thy God in vain; for the LORD will not hold him guiltless that taketh his name in vain."[38]

The God of Abraham believes in personal relationships—one on one. All the complex hierarchies and apostolic successions that we have invented in this world amount to nothing more than long strings of cold and powerless rumors that God disdains.[39] They are dead bodies—like well-dressed corpses laid out at a funeral home. If we could be saved by group associations Judas Iscariot would not be burning in Hell today.[40] Until we know the God of Abraham personally, we would be wise to leave his name out of our business. Tossing his name around only fans the flames of his righteous anger. He hates pretenses, and this one especially. It is blasphemy.

Every one of the commandments is given for our benefit. If God did not care about us, he would not communicate with us at all, and he certainly would not give us any commandments about our personal life.[41] He gave us written commands so that we can focus our lives well and experience our true potential.[42] The law reveals our burden of sin and positions us to shed that burden; it never adds anything to it.[43]

The effective goal of God's law is our freedom, and the Fourth Commandment illustrates that well. It says, "Remember the sabbath day, to keep it holy. Six days shalt thou labour, and do all thy work: But the seventh day is the sabbath of the LORD thy God: in it thou shalt not do any work, thou, nor thy son, nor thy daughter, thy manservant, nor thy maidservant, nor thy cattle, nor thy stranger that is within thy gates: For in six days the LORD made heaven and earth, the sea, and all that in them is, and rested the seventh day: wherefore the LORD blessed the sabbath day, and hallowed it."[44]

Notice that one day per week is set aside for rest. We are literally commanded to take a break and rest in Jehovah—who ultimately provides everything.[45]

So to recap the first four commandments: we as individuals are told to have Jehovah and no other gods before him, we are told not to make idols, we are told not to use God's name in vain, and we are told to rest thoroughly one day of the week. These first four commandments focus on our relationship with God.

So in order to have a good relationship with the God of Abraham we must have him before all others and rest in him. The two commandments between those tell us what not to do, so that we can head in that right direction. This could not be any simpler to understand, and it seems incredibly easy to do. But doing this is not easy at all. In fact, it is nearly impossible.

Larger than life

What would keep us from accepting Jehovah and resting in him for a day each week? Usually just one five letter word—pride. Perhaps even more ironic is the fact that this same trait will make it impossible for us to avoid violating the Second and Third Commandments as well. With the help of pride it is impossible for us *not* to do these things![46] We cannot avoid making idols and abusing the name of God; it comes as naturally as swimming to ducks.

That is bad news! But we need to hear it because it is true. We know intuitively that blasphemy and false images of God are wrong, but we just keep coming back to them by nature. There is a gap between what we know is right, and what we are by nature.[47] You can't fix that gap.[48] But what we can do is admit that the problem is real and lay our root of pride on the butcher block of the cross below the razor edge of the Ten Commandments. We can allow God's laws to shred our self-righteous pride and expose it for what it is—a sugary lie right out of the pit.[49]

Cultures around the world are chock full of self-righteous pride. When we try to get a grip on this we learn a little more about the surprisingly slick nature of pride. Pride is a master of camouflage and mimicry that can easily put a flexible octopus to shame, but it has such a powerful influence on our lives that it slips out into plain sight constantly.[50] Pride is like a gallon of milk soaked deep into the back seats of your car—they may be clean on the surface, but when the hot weather comes there will be no hiding it. Like pride its smell is larger-than-life and helps no one.

The final solution

There is a broad spectrum of ways to dress up our evils, but there is only one solution to the root problem. Dressing up a corpse for a funeral service may help friends to remember a life, but those clothes will do nothing to restore the life that was lost. Death cannot be solved with nice garments.[51]

Those trained in CPR can often resuscitate a person whose heart has suddenly stopped beating, but it is not a matter of dressing them up. In fact, quickly exposing the chest is standard procedure if an AED is used. These are emergency procedures for everyone to learn because when a person's blood suddenly stops circulating, waiting 10 minutes for paramedics to arrive is often too long.

In warm air a body declines rapidly. After 20 minutes without blood flow, a healthy resuscitation is rare. The brain cells break down quickly, and within a few hours there is absolutely no chance of return. Bacteria begin to break down the organs, and within a few days the natural decay of a body smells awful. Funeral homes usually keep bodies cool and embalm them to slow this natural process, but there is no way to recover their lives.[52]

We do not like to think about this impossible barricade of death, but there is great hope in seeing it with open eyes. Life is an amazing treasure, and through observing death we are reminded that this treasure we enjoy is an absolute gift that we could never replace.[53] The irreversible death and decay of a person's body proves his self-made arguments foolish, and it leaves us with no realistic foundation for our lives other than grace.[54]

The insightful woman who anointed Jesus of Nazareth with a pound of spikenard knew this well. Mary of Bethany saw the grace needed for her life more clearly when her brother Lazarus passed away. He had been critically ill leading up to his death, and Mary and Martha sent a message to Jesus hoping to get some help. But after receiving the message, Jesus waited for two more days before going to Bethany.[55]

Lazarus died while Jesus of Nazareth waited, and by the time Jesus arrived in Bethany, Lazarus had been dead for four days. Mary came out to meet Jesus, and in tears she said, "Lord, if thou hadst been here, my brother had not died." After Jesus saw Mary and others with her weeping, he asked where they had placed Lazarus' body, and they responded, "Lord, come and see." At that point Jesus himself wept.

The body of Lazarus was placed in a hollow grave sealed with a large stone. Jesus commanded the group that was there to remove the stone, and Martha quickly objected. She knew that her brother's body had begun to decay in the heat, and she did not want to dishonor his memory with such an awful smell. But Jesus reminded her saying, "Said I not unto thee, that, if thou wouldest believe, thou shouldest see the glory of God?"

While fighting the foul stench of death, the group there went ahead and removed the stone. Then Jesus spoke out, "Father, I thank thee that thou hast heard me. And I knew that thou hearest me always: but because of the people which stand by I said it, that they may believe that thou hast sent me." After that, he cried with a loud voice, "Lazarus, come forth."

And that is exactly what happened. The man that had been dead and decaying came out with grave clothes wrapped around his hands and feet, and there was a napkin wrapped over his face. Then Jesus had some very practical advice for the group that witnessed this. He said, "Loose him, and let him go." It was time for Lazarus to shed those grave clothes and live freely.

We would all love to witness such an event, but this small miracle was only an object lesson to teach about the true miracle of the Messiah's ministry—the one that every one of us can experience. Human life is certainly a miracle in its own right, and completely salvaging a decaying human body is impressive, but the Messiah came for a much bigger mission. Mary saw her decaying brother brought back to life by Jesus of Nazareth, and she realized that what she saw was the visible tip of a much larger substance. He showed his power over death in order to illustrate his ability to save the human spirit.[56]

A human body begins as a single cell and grows in the womb of a mother, then beyond. This process of growth that takes place is fascinating. The human body is a collection of mass that is no different from the dirt and minerals in a vegetable garden,[57] but a body is formed as a natural process following a written plan inside the initial cell.[58] The way that the elements are arranged makes all the difference between an ordinary soil and an extraordinary human body—illustrating well the amazing power of order and the principle of emergence.

The development of a human body is a chain reaction like a set of falling dominoes. But instead of toppling a neat little line of tiles, the preset elements interact with natural materials of many sorts to build a unified body with trillions of functional components. It is an amazing chain of action that shows an obvious and very impressive foresight.[59] The arms and legs, the hands and feet, the eyes and ears, the heart and lungs, the blood and brain all form out of common elements. And we call the thing that is formed a body.[60]

The growth that takes place inside of a womb is preparing a tiny person for freedom outside of the womb. The legs that are forming cannot walk inside the womb, the vocal cords cannot speak there, the eyes see little or nothing on that side, and yet all these things are initially formed in the womb.[61]

When a living person leaves the womb he or she begins stretching out—gently at first, then over days and months more confidently. This unique stretching and exploring of a new human being is a pleasure for happy parents to watch. No two infants will follow the same path, but they all tend to be going places.

Parents will often move things to protect a newly mobile infant; but as a child grows and begins toddling around, less and less is out of reach. Inevitably a child must be taught some things.[62] Leaving children to educate themselves without any leadership is not wise. And if we do allow them to blossom on their own, we should not be too surprised if we find that the tender little bud has blossomed into a steely monster.[63] When we work hard to provide every whim for our children, they will tend to work us only harder.[64]

Patiently teaching children to appreciate what they have will bring much more value into their lives than indulging and spoiling them ever will.[65] We are each stewards of everything that we have—including our individual mind and body.[66] We are managing these things that are on loan to us, and the great irony of this fact is that we are not especially good at doing that.[67] We all tend to waste a lot of what we manage. Each of us needs to be taught how to genuinely appreciate our opportunities, and that requires a personal grasp of the truth.

Mary of Bethany smelled the awful stench of her brother's decaying body, but she also sensed something very profound through that harsh experience. She saw the death of her brother's body as a glaring illustration of human ambitions with no enduring purpose. It was a whiff of her own dead spirit and a sharp reminder of her profound guilt in the eyes of God. So when Jesus of Nazareth raised her brother from the dead, Mary found a new and bolder hope— that her spirit could also be salvaged and that she could know God personally and live with him honestly.[68] She appreciated the spirit of what Jesus was doing and gripped the deeper truth that he embodies.

The Messiah came to do more than heal bodies; he came to heal our lives forever.[69] There is something about watching a brother or friend lose a battle against a terminal illness that is both sobering and intensifying. Even with all the medical resources of our time, there are always conditions that cannot be cured, bodies that cannot be healed. Mary watched helplessly as an illness destroyed her brother's body; and as she watched, she saw herself vividly, saw a chilling picture of her own potential wasting away. That experience illustrated something very sacred to her.

Mary of Bethany had a problem that she refused to understate.[70] No medicine or expertise on earth would ever solve it, but she saw a true solution in the body of Jesus. Jesus of Nazareth had restored the body of her brother, but his own body was built to be crucified for her and others—to crush death once for all. And she knew it.

Like every other Jew, Mary knew that her sin required a substitute. But it bothered her deeply that none of the animal sacrifices that took place in Jerusalem were final.[71] There was a steady stream of blood being poured out at the temple, and it continued for years upon years. Each time she saw the sacrifice it would help ease her conscience somewhat, but the relief she felt was always slight and temporary.

The logic of having a substitute was simple and sound, but how could lambs and goats ever take Mary's place justly? The animals did not understand her sin at all, and of course they never chose to die on her behalf. Like all of us, Mary had committed wrongs that she could never right. The required sacrifices allowed her to express her weary conscience somewhat, but they were only a symbol of what was right. They did not actually balance the scales.[72]

But Mary also saw something that many other Jews refused to look at. Indeed, she had sinned against God and hurt others; but the deeper issue—the root of those wrongs—was her own heart and soul.[73] If by some miracle she could repair every sin that she had ever done, the source of her sin would continue to bear its fruit. She needed to mend her trail of wreckage, certainly; but even more importantly, she needed new life that she had never had before.[74]

That rough prophet, John the Baptist, who had drawn large crowds out into the deserts of Judea had spoken distinctly of this other cleansing, and his whole public ministry was a preparation for it. John had spoken much about repenting—that we should go back and get things right with God. Using the Jordan River and other local bodies of water, John publicly immersed many volunteers from his audience, graphically showing the need for this moral cleansing.[75] But he knew that this baptism was symbolic of another event that needed to take place. He knew that the true event involved a spiritual immersion—one that would cleanse the heart and breathe life into lifeless spirits.[76]

Jesus of Nazareth was born into this world to do that work—to reconcile us to the Father.[77] Any other person who would willingly give his life to redeem your soul would not be effective. You cannot get a drink out of a dry cup, and the bound are not free to free us. But the Messiah was sent as a gift from God.[78] He was not born with Adam's nature but by the power of God. Mary of Nazareth was overshadowed by "the power of the Highest,"[79] and God himself placed the Messiah in her womb.

Jesus of Nazareth was born with the perfect sinless flesh of God,[80] formed from an imperfect mother and by the only perfect Father. God formed one perfect cell—with a living soul and a living spirit—who would prove to be the one perfect Messiah.[81] He is literally the author of time and transcends it. He grew in the womb of his chosen mother, was born, and grew into a man who would freely lay down his life for us all. He was sent for that purpose and, in doing so, he fulfilled scores of Jewish prophecies.[82]

Mary of Bethany craved a clean spirit, and that is exactly what Jesus of Nazareth provides. She knew that he would lay down his life as a perfect substitute for her sins and ours, and the spikenard oil that she had poured on him was to anoint him for that burial. As his body was being buried the body of our sins was being buried also, but there was a great promise of life to look forward to as well.[83]

After he was betrayed by a close friend and arrested in the Garden of Gethsemane, Jesus had a very unjust trial, was beaten horrifically, and was led out to a place called Calvary.[84] There the Romans crucified him by nailing his feet and the base of his hands to a rough wooden cross and leaving him to die a slow agonizing death. But the burden that Jesus carried that day was not the pain of the cross, it was the weight of the world. He carried the burden of every vile sin in human history, including mine and yours.[85] He gave himself freely as a substitute for all who had ever lived and all who ever would.

About three dark hours after noon, Jesus had finished the work of substitution. He said profoundly, "It is finished."[86] Just before he died, he cried out with a loud voice, and an earthquake followed. Then he yielded up his own spirit—the ghost of his body—to the work of his Father. The presence of Jesus was so powerful that the hardened Roman centurion who oversaw the crucifixion admitted, "Truly this was the Son of God."[87]

Standing by the cross that day were three women who shared an identical first name. The Gospel of John records, "Now there stood by the cross of Jesus his mother, and his mother's sister, Mary the wife of Cleophas, and Mary Magdalene."[88] The Jews had been

eagerly anticipating the birth of the Messiah for
centuries, and the prophecies of Daniel had pinpointed
the time.[89] The name Mary—meaning bitter—had
become a common one, and these women illustrated the
bitter spirits of many who would be made alive by the
work of the Messiah.

  Joseph of Arimathaea was another who stood
by the cross that day. He was an unlikely disciple of
Jesus, but a very sincere one. Joseph was a man with
more resources than most, but he was not blinded by his
assets. He saw how worthless his things were relative to
the body of the Messiah. He had the treasure of Jesus'
words in his heart, and this man was truly rich. He
longed to honor the body of his deceased friend and
Savior. And the book of Matthew tells us that this rich
man went to the governor of Judea and "begged the
body of Jesus."[90]

  One of the Roman soldiers had already run a
spear into Jesus' side to confirm his death; and once the
centurion certified it with the governor, Joseph was
given permission to prepare the body for burial. Joseph
returned to the cross with some fine linen he had
purchased, and a friend met him there with several
gallons of an antiseptic mixture composed of fresh aloe
gel and fragrant myrrh oil.[91] They carried the body from
the cross and rubbed the mixture into the wounds to
sterilize them. Once it was washed with the mixture,
they wrapped the body in the fine linens and laid it in a

tomb that he had carved out of rock on his land nearby. They sealed the opening with a large stone and left.

But the crucifixion of this man was more than another cruel injustice. Human history records an ocean of injustices, but none like this. Jesus of Nazareth came on a mission to solve the inherent problem of humanity, and he did! We all died in Adam, but in Jesus—the Messiah—we can all be made truly alive and free.[92]

More than ever

They placed the body of Jesus in the tomb that evening. But the Messiah's work was not limited by his death—it was expanded.[93] He died for us so that we can be forgiven of our sins. And he gave his life as a ransom for our lives so that we have the power to break free from the prison of our sin nature.[94] His body took the sin of the world and carried it, then after three days he rose from the dead—showing the complete triumph of his work and his rightful authority to cleanse us thoroughly.[95]

Mary of Bethany craved forgiveness that she could not afford, but she needed more than that. She needed salvation. More than a clean slate, she needed a new nature—a fresh smell to her spirit that she had never had before. This is what the resurrection of Jesus provides. He gave us an honest way to let go of our old sins, and much more than that: he gave us a complete provision for new life moving forward. When the blood of Jesus pays on our account, it pays deeply and changes our very nature, our identity, everything.[96]

Jesus is salvation. He is a person we can know—that we need to know in order to live whole and free. Salvation is not a prayer; it is a person. The Jewish Scriptures taught this long before Mary of Nazareth gave birth to the Messiah. Isaiah said, "Behold, thy salvation cometh; behold, his reward is with him, and his work before him."[97] Jeremiah prophesied, "And ye shall seek me, and find me, when ye shall search for me with all your heart."[98]

Jesus of Nazareth confirmed these prophecies with his own words. He said, "I am the bread of life: he that cometh to me shall never hunger; and he that believeth on me shall never thirst."[99] He said, "And this is life eternal, that they might know thee the only true God, and Jesus Christ, whom thou hast sent."[100] We see the words of Jesus in the Scripture, but we must come to him personally before we can have his life in us. He said, "Search the scriptures; for in them ye think ye have eternal life: and they are they which testify of me. And ye will not come to me, that ye might have life."[101]

There is no prophet, no pope, and no pastor who can tell you if you know God. Jesus said, "My sheep hear my voice, and I know them, and they follow me: And I give unto them eternal life; and they shall never perish, neither shall any man pluck them out of my hand."[102] There are plenty of other voices in this world that would happily confirm you in their system and add your name to their growing inventory. But your forever will be no better for it.

When you hear the voice of God, it will ring loud and true in your conscience and will align precisely with the words that he has written down for us in his scriptures.[103] But these are not to be confused. Reading his words is not the same as hearing his voice and actually knowing him. If we do not know his voice personally, we cannot be following him personally. It is that simple: "He that hath the Son hath life; and he that hath not the Son of God hath not life."[104] Jesus said, "Come unto me, all ye that labour and are heavy laden, and I will give you rest."[105]

You can do many things in this life without knowing God, and the American rock climber Alex Honnold is a great example of that. When he did his free solo of El Capitan, Honnold overcame a wall that many thought was impossible. He maintains high standards that would put some monks to shame and considers himself "basically Mormon" in terms of wholesome living, but he has also defined himself as a militant atheist. He memorized many of the intricate details of El Capitan and had courage enough to climb it with no safety equipment while choosing to live ignorant of his own Creator.

But there is another wall that no amount of passion or training will ever overcome. It is the wall that separates us from our Creator.[106] We are dead to him, and he is dead to us until that wall is removed. You cannot remove that wall. You cannot tunnel through it. You cannot climb over it. And there is no amount of religious activity that will help.[107] Using good works to prove ourselves right is like a serial killer feeling justified because for 300 days of the year he was living a fairly normal life. Good works are not a bartering tool to God. They are standard procedure.[108]

We can do all kinds of good deeds without knowing God, but they are only an insult to his standards.[109] If I were to steal your car and bring you a bouquet of pretty dandelions with it once in a while, would you be impressed by my thoughtfulness? Yet we reject the voice of the Messiah and tell God why he should be impressed with our own "wonderful works."[110] It is absolute foolishness, and God hates it. Jesus said, "If therefore the light that is in thee be darkness, how great is that darkness!"[111]

There is a solid foundation that we can build our lives on. It is not the loose clay and shifting sands that Rowling called "rock bottom." It is a real foundation that will endure the storms of this life and the righteous judgment of God after this life. It is the foundation of Jesus Christ—laid down for us.[112]

Healthy relationships rely on good faith. There is a time and place for verifying, but at some point we need to build on the things we know. We do not need more evidence, we need to embrace the evidence that we have. The Ten Commandments were written in stone to silence our every excuse, and they do so very effectively "that every mouth may be stopped, and all the world may become guilty before God."[113] No one ever rejects the Messiah for a lack of evidence. The one who has designed your life and body from a single cell in your mother's womb is worthy of your confidence moving forward.

When Jesus of Nazareth died on the cross, an amazing thing happened inside the temple in Jerusalem: the huge veil concealing the most holy place was torn from the top to the bottom.[114] Jesus had "broken down the middle wall of partition"[115] and made it possible for us to have perfect peace with God. That healthy relationship is not possible, however, until we stop trying to prove ourselves worthy of him. We are not worthy. That is the whole point of the Messiah coming. He came to help us and to correct our wrongs—to show us grace that we could never deserve. The one who formed you from the womb is the only one worthy to shape your life moving forward.

You are truly the master of your own destiny because God has given you free will. The choice of destiny is yours to make. But you will hate that destiny if you fail to place your life in the hands of the true Master. This is the great irony of all time. You have to die to your own natural ambitions to find real life. Jesus said, "For whosoever will save his life shall lose it: and whosoever will lose his life for my sake shall find it."[116] We live in an amazing reality, but why? Where are you going from here?

Just as the soil of a vegetable garden can form a powerful human body when guided by a genetic plan, so we can become part of the body of Christ by following his plan. We can work with him that closely, if we will accept the truth that he brought us. Through his wisdom "we are members of his body, of his flesh, and of his bones."[117] He takes individuals like Abraham, Isaac, and Jacob and builds their lives into something impossible by human standards. Like the engineered pieces of a computer that fit together with precision, so God fits us together as only he knows how.

Receiving Christ may not come easily, however. It should be easy, but pride dies very hard. Susan Polgar's little sister Judit would one day defeat her at chess and go on to become the greatest female chess player of all time. Yet Judit says that her "whole life has become richer," not through chess, but through giving her life in marriage and motherhood. She saw the beauty of putting her life in the hands of another by faith, and she was right. But what has she done with Jesus of Nazareth?

These sisters are Jewish, but that does not mean they have received the Jewish Messiah. The rejection that Jesus of Nazareth experienced in the 1st century continues right now. He laid down his life for the world, but many even of his own family—the Jews—have rejected him.[118]

In order to receive the Messiah, we have to recognize that we are in a very desperate condition without him. If there were any other way for us to make it without the blood of Jesus, he would not have taken our sin to the cross. He prayed "if it be possible, let this cup pass from me."[119] There was no other way. His blood was the only way for us to be made right with the Father and to join his family by adoption.

Jesus of Nazareth gave himself for each of us; we just receive the gift. It is that simple. But it is not easy. We cannot appreciate the gift—or actually receive it—until we see the need for it.

A man once had a very nice Mustang sports car that was taken off the road and set under a tree for years. It began to get filthy and rust. The man lost the car's value because he failed to see it, and the opportunity slipped away from him.

The gift of God was given to breathe life into our spirits. Salvation is not fire insurance; it is not a get out of jail free card; and it is not an excuse to live lawlessly. Salvation gives us the power to break the chains of sin and to love God sincerely.[120] Jesus did not give his life primarily so that we can avoid hell when we die, and he certainly did not give his life so that we can be unruly; he gave his life so that we can have life.[121] He said, "I am come that they might have life, and that they might have it more abundantly."[122]

Yes, we will avoid the wrath of God by receiving his gift.[123] But that's not the primary point of what he did. It is a secondary result. I do not kiss my wife to avoid being slapped by her, but because I love her. Salvation that looks like fire insurance is not the salvation that Jesus gave his life for, and it will not pay out on the day of judgment. It is a huge violation of the first commandment.[124] Salvation does free us from the wrath of God—including the fury of an eternal hell— but far more importantly it allows us to love him sincerely and work with him well.

We all hate dealing with the consequences of our sin, but salvation is only effective for those who hate being sinners. We look at the violence and evil of Jesus' crucifixion and say in our heart, "That is how vile my own sin is, and I hate what I am without Jesus of Nazareth! If he had not done that, my spirit could never live!" It is simple and honest to do this, yet few are willing to do it. Few are willing to receive him for who he is.[125]

The Gospel of John says of Jesus: "He came unto his own, and his own received him not. But as many as received him, to them gave he power to become the sons of God, even to them that believe on his name: Which were born, not of blood, nor of the will of the flesh, nor of the will of man, but of God."[126]

His blood can strengthen us deeply. When we receive him, he receives us as family.

Ashwin, the young man who sat beside me on that flight from Fiji, realized that he needed new strength that he had never found in Hinduism. He saw his guilt through the Law of Moses and knew that the hope he needed was hope that he could never deserve. Ashwin needed to get adopted through the blood of Jesus, and that is what he sought in his prayers that day. He needed a new heart and to be received by grace. And if he sought it earnestly, we can be sure that he—like millions of others throughout history—found it all.

The Book of Romans describes this adoption, saying, "For ye have not received the spirit of bondage again to fear; but ye have received the Spirit of adoption, whereby we cry, Abba, Father."[127] The Father does not give us the spirit of fear, "but of power, and of love, and of a sound mind."[128] It is the Spirit of *adoption* that puts us at ease. We become so secure in his hands that we can call him our Abba—like an infant just learning his first sounds.

And this Spirit of adoption that the Father extends to us becomes our new standard procedure. We begin to love and adopt others around us like we never have before, and this is the living heart of the body of Christ. We love as he loved because of his Spirit of adoption in us. Jesus said, "By this shall all men know that ye are my disciples, if ye have love one to another."[129]

Saving grace gives us a new heart and teaches us how to truly walk with God. The book of Titus says, "For the grace of God that bringeth salvation hath appeared to all men, Teaching us that, denying ungodliness and worldly lusts, we should live soberly, righteously, and godly, in this present world."[130]

Paul—a faithful Jew who received Jesus while traveling to Damascus one day—wrote to the church at Corinth, "Therefore if any man be in Christ, he is a new creature: old things are passed away; behold, all things are become new."[131]

This is the key to living beyond your natural end. We could go on discussing what it means to receive this gift and know him personally, but "faith cometh by hearing, and hearing by the word of God."[132] The best thing to do is get a copy of God's Word (Authorized Version) and study it.

You can use the endnotes in this little book to find helpful passages that relate to the topics we looked at, and the book of Romans is also a great place to start reading. You can also find helpful resources at www.onesoulatatime.net. Talk to God about this and ask for wisdom. There are good local churches around the world, and www.fundamental.org is an easy place to start looking for one. Do what you can and ask help for what you can't. Go further!

STUDY NOTE:

Personal study is the shoe leather of good progress. If we care, we study. There is no greater opportunity afforded to us in this life than to study the very Word of God and to thrive by it spiritually. The King James Bible is the only Authorized Version of God's Word in English and has stood out as the clear international authority for centuries. To maximize the benefit of study time and avoid needless confusion it is highly recommended that the following Bible references be studied in the Authorized Version. May the living God deeply bless your continuing study in the days ahead.

CHAPTER 1

1 Proverbs 16:24
  Ecclesiastes 12:10-11
  Luke 21:33
2 Numbers 13:31-14:2
3 Proverbs 29:18
4 Proverbs 12:18
  Ezekiel 20:18
5 Psalm 9:9
  Psalm 27:5
  Psalm 40:2
6 Genesis 2:7
  I Corinthians 15:45
7 Psalm 139:14
8 Luke 12:6-7
9 Titus 1:15
10 Proverbs 24:30-32
11 Proverbs 29:27
12 Romans 1:19
13 Proverbs 16:32
14 Ecclesiastes 6:1-4
15 Matthew 12:35
16 Luke 6:44-45
17 Matthew 23:25
18 Proverbs 5:6
19 John 12:35
20 Genesis 24:63
21 Genesis 2:3
22 Psalm 119:105
23 Psalm 119:99
24 Psalm 4:4
25 Mark 4:18-19
26 James 1:22-25
27 Proverbs 4:26
28 1 Corinthians 13:11
29 Proverbs 13:14-15
30 Psalm 40:2
31 Proverbs 4:19
32 Jeremiah 17:9
33 Philippians 4:8
34 Proverbs 30:5
35 Matthew 7:7
36 Psalm 119:9-11
37 Mark 7:6
38 Proverbs 4:23
39 I Thessalonians 5:18
40 Ecclesiastes 9:4
41 Luke 19:1-10
42 Matthew 16:26
43 Luke 12:15
44 Matthew 6:19-20
45 Matthew 18:3
46 Ecclesiastes 21:1
47 Deuteronomy 34:7
48 Genesis 29:20
49 Luke 16:10-12

CHAPTER 2

1 Proverbs 12:15
2 1 Corinthians 3:18
3 Proverbs 28:13
4 Matthew 7:26
5 1 Samuel 15:23
6 Psalm 9:15
7 Luke 6:47-48
8 Proverbs 20:27
9 Matthew 6:22-23
10 Galatians 6:3
11 Ecclesiastes 8:11
12 Job 42:6
13 Ephesians 2:1-3
14 Matthew 19:7
15 Luke 6:41
16 John 8:44
17 Romans 2:1
18 Matthew 23:29-31
19 Romans 7:24
20 Ecclesiastes 7:20
21 John 8:32
22 Philippians 2:13
23 Galatians 6:7
24 Acts 20:35
25 Matthew 9:36
26 Proverbs 18:24
27 Galatians 6:2
28 Isaiah 53:4-6
29 Matthew 8:16-17
30 Ezra 9:13-15
31 Luke 17:2
32 Revelation 18:7-8
33 Numbers 11:12-14
34 Job 6:25
James 2:26
35 Psalm 19:1
36 Proverbs 16:11
37 Psalm 139:14
38 Matthew 10:30
39 Mark 8:37
40 Psalm 139:17
41 Matthew 16:26
42 Genesis 21:1-7
43 Genesis 25:21
44 Genesis 30:1
45 Genesis 37:2-4
46 Genesis 37:5-8
47 Genesis 37:9-11
48 Genesis 37:12-19
49 Genesis 37:20-27
50 Genesis 39:1-6
51 Genesis 39:7-10
52 Genesis 39:11-20
53 Genesis 39:21-23
54 Genesis 41:1-4
55 Genesis 41:15-24
56 Genesis 41:25-27
57 Genesis 41:28-44

58 Proverbs 12:27
59 Romans 8:28
60 Genesis 41:47-53
61 Genesis 41:54-42:6
62 Genesis 42:7-9
63 Genesis 42:10-17
64 Genesis 42:18-20
65 Genesis 42:21-24
66 Genesis 42:24-26
67 Genesis 42:36-38
68 Genesis 43:1-4

69 Genesis 43:16-34
70 Genesis 44:1-2
71 Genesis 44:3-12
72 Genesis 44:13-14
73 Genesis 44:15-17
74 Genesis 44:18-34
75 Genesis 45:1-5
76 Genesis 45:14-15
77 Genesis 46:29-30
78 James 5:16
79 Matthew 5:44-45

CHAPTER 3

1 Luke 12:33-34
2 Matthew 15:3-6
3 Mark 7:9
4 2 Corinthians 4:18
5 Psalm 24:3-4
6 Isaiah 44:17-18
7 Luke 11:9-10
8 1 Kings 3:5-12
9 1 Kings 3:16-22
10 1 Kings 3:23-27
11 Proverbs 22:20-21
12 Ephesians 4:32
13 Mark 5:26
14 John 8:9
15 Romans 2:15
16 I Timothy 4:2
   Titus 1:15

17 Ecclesiastes 2:1-11
18 Exodus 31:17
   Deuteronomy 9:10
19 Hebrews 4:12
20 Romans 3:19
   James 2:10
21 Exodus 20:3-17
22 Isaiah 65:1-2
23 1 John 3:16
24 Psalm 19:7-9
25 Proverbs 17:17
26 Psalm 35:14
27 Jeremiah 29:11
28 Galatians 3:21-24
29 John 4:3-42
30 Psalm 119:105
31 Daniel 9:25-26

[32] Hebrews 9:7-14
Hebrews 10:11-13
[33] Proverbs 6:23
[34] Isaiah 60:18
Isaiah 62:11
[35] Matthew 1:21
[36] Mark 2:15-16
[37] Mark 2:17
[38] Romans 10:3
[39] John 1:10-11
[40] 2 Corinthians 11:14
[41] Romans 3:3-4

[42] Romans 3:20
[43] Luke 7:47
[44] Isaiah 1:18
[45] Matthew 3:1-6
[46] John 11:1,5
[47] Luke 10:38-42
[48] Exodus 15:23
Ruth 1:20
[49] Matthew 26:6-13
John 12:1-8
Mark 14:3-9
[50] Matthew 26:14-16

CHAPTER 4

[1] Psalm 139:13-14
[2] Corinthians 4:17
[3] James 2:26
[4] James 4:14
[5] John 8:36
[6] John 8:33
[7] John 8:34
[8] 2 Timothy 1:9
[9] Ephesians 4:16
[10] 1 Corinthians 14:40
[11] 1 John 3:4
[12] Romans 1:20
[13] Hebrews 12:16
[14] Proverbs 14:9
[15] Psalm 1:6
[16] Romans 6:23

[17] Romans 8:22
[18] Romans 5:12
[19] Genesis 2:16-17
[20] 1 Corinthians 15:22
[21] Ecclesiastes 9:18
[22] Matthew 7:13-14
[23] 1 Corinthians 12:18-21
[24] Isaiah 57:17
[25] Exodus 24:12
[26] Exodus 20:2
[27] Exodus 1:13-14
[28] Exodus 1:11
[29] Luke 12:7
[30] Genesis 1:27
[31] Exodus 20:3
[32] 1 John 2:15-17

[33] Exodus 20:4-6
[34] Deuteronomy 5:9
[35] Romans 6:15
[36] 1 John 5:3
[37] John 14:15
[38] Exodus 20:7
[39] Mark 7:6-9
[40] John 17:12
[41] Deuteronomy 5:29
[42] Deuteronomy 4:40
[43] Romans 3:20-22
[44] Exodus 20:8-11
[45] Philippians 4:19
[46] 2 Timothy 3:1-2
[47] Ephesians 2:2-3
[48] Ephesians 2:12-13
   2 Samuel 14:14
[49] Isaiah 64:6
[50] Isaiah 3:9
[51] Matthew 23:27
[52] Hebrews 9:27
   Job 14:11-12
[53] 1 Corinthians 4:7
[54] 1 Corinthians 15:10
[55] John 11:1-45
[56] John 11:25
[57] Genesis 2:7
[58] Psalm 139:16
[59] Isaiah 44:24
[60] 1 Corinthians 12:14
[61] Jeremiah 1:5

[62] Proverbs 9:9
[63] Proverbs 29:15
[64] 1 Samuel 3:12-13
[65] 1 Timothy 6:6
[66] 1 Corinthians 15:38
[67] Luke 16:11-12
[68] Ezekiel 36:26
[69] John 6:47
[70] Ezekiel 37:1-3
[71] Hebrews 10:1-3
[72] Hebrews 10:4
[73] Matthew 12:34
[74] John 3:36
[75] Mark 1:3-5
[76] Matthew 3:11
[77] 2 Corinthians 5:18
   Ephesians 2:16
[78] John 3:16
[79] Luke 1:35
[80] 2 Corinthians 5:21
   Luke 1:47
[81] 1 Timothy 2:5
[82] Luke 24:25
[83] Romans 6:4-6
[84] John 19:1-3
   Luke 23:33
[85] 1 John 2:2
[86] John 19:30
[87] Matthew 27:54
[88] John 19:25
[89] Daniel 9:26

90 Matthew 27:57-58
91 John 19:38-39
92 1 Corinthians 15:22
93 Hebrews 10:10
94 Galatians 6:14-15
95 1 Corinthians 15:3-4
   Colossians 2:14-15
96 John 3:6-7
97 Isaiah 62:11
98 Jeremiah 29:13
99 John 6:35
100 John 17:3
101 John 5:39-40
102 John 10:27-28
103 Psalm 12:6
104 1 John 5:12
105 Matthew 11:28
106 Isaiah 59:2
107 Romans 5:6
108 1 John 1:5
109 Malachi 1:8
110 Matthew 7:22
111 Matthew 6:23
112 1 Corinthians 3:11
113 Romans 3:19
114 Matthew 27:51
115 Ephesians 2:14
116 Matthew 16:25
117 Ephesians 5:30
118 Isaiah 53:3
119 Matthew 26:39

120 1 John 1:6-7
121 Titus 2:11-14
122 John 10:10
123 Romans 5:9
    1 Thessalonians 1:10
124 Matthew 22:37-38
125 Luke 13:23-27
126 John 1:11-13
127 Romans 8:15
128 2 Timothy 1:7
129 John 13:35
130 Titus 2:11-12
131 2 Corinthians 5:17
132 Romans 10:17